The 2020 DC/Maryland Directory of Search Firms and Recruiters

Job Hunting? Get Your Resume in the Right Hands

Selected from
Custom Databanks'
Executive Search System™ Database

www.CustomDatabanks.com

The Executive Search System™

The 2020 DC/Maryland Directory of Search Firms and Recruiters
Selected from Custom Databanks' Executive Search System™ Database
www.CustomDatabanks.com

This Directory is sold subject to the condition that it shall not, by way of trade or otherwise, be lent, resold, hired our or otherwise circulated without the publisher's prior consent in any form whatsoever. You may not make any changes or modifications to this Directory or the data contained herein. You may not decompile, disassemble, or otherwise reverse engineer this Directory. You may not sub-license, rent, lend, lease, donate, sell, load, pledge, transfer, or distribute on a temporary or permanent basis any of the data contained in this Directory to another person or company.

Title to the data contained in this Directory is retained by Custom Databanks, Inc. and is not transferred to any user by grant of a license as provided. **You may not sell or further license this Directory or its data to any other person or organization without the express written permission of Custom Databanks, Inc.**

Copyright © 2020 Custom Databanks, Inc.
All Rights Reserved

The Executive Search System™

**The 2020 DC/Maryland Directory of Search Firms and Recruiters
Selected from Custom Databanks' Executive Search System™ Database**
www.CustomDatabanks.com

Table of Contents

Chapter		Page
Chapter 1	Introduction	5
Chapter 2	The Directory	7
Chapter 3	Appendix – Note	75
Chapter 4	Appendix - About The Data	75

Chapter 1: Introduction

Introduction

Job hunters need to do many things to get a job - - call all their friends and relatives, answer ads, and send out hundreds, even thousands of letters and resumes in a targeted direct email, direct fax or direct snail mail campaign. Our online databases and directories are designed to help you in that last task - to get your personal cover letter and resume to the executive search firms that specialize in your field.

Executive search firms work to fill management positions at top companies across the U.S. and abroad. It is estimated that almost two-thirds of executive positions are filled by executive search firms. Personnel agencies work to fill professional, technical, and administrative personnel at companies. The search firms and agencies in our database are hired and paid by companies that need new employees.

*The **2020 DC/Maryland Directory of Search Firms and Recruiters** is drawn from our database of more than 16,000 search firms and personnel agencies and more than 38,000 key contacts. We selected firms that are located in the District of Columbia and Maryland for this directory.*

The companies are arranged alphabetically by name with multiple offices of the same firm listed alphabetically by city.

Our Directories contain full contact information and descriptions for each firm in its category.

About Custom Databanks, Inc.

Custom Databanks, Inc. has been publishing databases for use on personal computers since 1987. We were the first company to offer recruiter data ready for use on PC diskettes. Our Executive Search System™ contains the names and addresses of 16,000+ top US and Canadian search firms and more than 38,000 key contacts. In addition, we publish the Venture Search System™ with data on 2,600+ top US and Canadian venture, private equity and investment firms and 9,500+ key contacts. We update our databases continuously, our online database weekly, and our directories annually.

We publish Directories of Executive Search Firms and Recruiters selected from our Executive Search System™ database. We publish Directories of Venture Capital and Private Equity Firms selected from our Venture Search System™ database. See http://www.customdatabanks.com/ebook-samples/ and http://www.customdatabanks.com/venture-capital-ebook/ for a complete list. Look for these Directories on Amazon.com and BarnesandNoble.com. You can download a free sample to your Kindle or Nook App to see information you can use in your job hunt.

In addition, users can download data by the record from our Search System™ databases. See http://customdatabanks.com/ss/email-distribution-one-time-download/ and http://customdatabanks.com/ss/vss-email-distribution-or-download/ for more information.

Our data are widely used by job hunters and career professionals. In addition to many internet sites and resume writers, many of the major professional outplacement companies (Career Partners, Drake Beam, Right Associates, Lee Hecht Harrison, Goodrich & Sherwood, . . .) and University career offices (Harvard, Stanford, Columbia) use Custom Databanks' data. You can explore our venture/PE database at no charge at http://customdatabanks.com/ss/vss-email-distribution-or-download/.

Custom Databanks' data are available for download by the record on the internet at http://www.customdatabanks.com and through resume writers, career coaches, outplacement companies, college career centers, and data suppliers. The databases are updated on a continuous basis, the web sites are updated weekly, and the Directories updated annually. The information Custom Databanks, Inc. provides is the most up-to-date and accurate available anywhere.

Chapter 2: The Directory

2020 DC/Maryland Directory of Search Firms and Recruiters
Alphabetically by Company Name

AETEA INFORMATION TECHNOLOGY, INC.

From the website: Since 1979, AETEA Information Technology has delivered IT Consulting Services to Fortune 500 companies in a wide range of industries. From the financial services and pharmaceutical industries to the government sector, manufacturing and consumer packaged goods, we work with our clients to understand their business problems so that we can deliver the right solution to meet each client's needs.

Minimum salary for assignments: $50,000
Contingency search
Industries: most industries, communications, telecommunications, consumer, consumer packaged goods, financial services, government, public administration, hi-tech, pharmaceuticals, drugs, biologicals
Positions: information technology, MIS, networks, LAN, WAN, interim, contract, temporary placement
www.aetea.com

1445 Research Boulevard, Suite 210
Rockville, MD 20850
301-721-4200/fax 301-721-1730
Mr. Mark Nugent, Vice President /MNugent@aetea.com
Ms. Kristine Sims, Technical Recruiter /KSims@aetea.com/ /industries GEN/CMM/CON/CPG/FIN/GOV/positions MIS/NET/TEM
Mr. Don Muse, Business Development Director /DMuse@aetea.com/ /industries GEN/CMM/CON/CPG/FIN/GOV/positions MIS/NET/TEM
Mr. Nick Carr, IT Recruiter /NCarr@aetea.com/ /industries GEN/CMM/CON/CPG/FIN/GOV/positions MIS/NET/TEM
Mr. Jory Rubenstein, Vice President /JRubenstein@aetea.com/ /industries GEN/CMM/CON/CPG/FIN/GOV/positions MIS/NET/TEM
Mr. Rohit Gomber, Technical Recruiter /RGomber@aetea.com/ /industries GEN/CMM/CON/CPG/FIN/GOV/positions MIS/NET/TEM

ATC HEALTHCARE SERVICES

From the website: Since 1982 ATC has been growing and providing "staffing wherever healthcare is provided" through our network of over 65 company-owned and Franchised locations. Today we continue to support our nurses, healthcare professionals and facilities with innovative programs and benefits unique to the industry. If you are a healthcare professional seeking a challenging career opportunity, apply now online; or, if you are a healthcare facility looking for innovative programs to resolve your staffing challenges, find solutions with ATC!

No minimum salary for assignments
Contingency search
Industries: healthcare, hospitals
Positions: administration, therapists, nursing, interim, contract, temporary placement
www.atchealthcare.com

1450 Mercantile Lane, Suite 243
Largo, MD 20774
301-772-9616/fax 301-772-9619
Mr. David Savitsky , Chief Executive Officer /DSavitsky@atchealthcare.com

---

ACERTITUDE

From the website: Acertitude is a top-tier executive search firm and talent solutions consultancy. We collaborate closely with organizations to provide solutions that help them attract, recruit, and retain the leaders of tomorrow, matching executives with organizations where they truly thrive. Expertise: * Consumer * Healthcare + Life Sciences * Industrial * Nonprofit + Foundations * Private Equity * Professional Services * Technology * Telecommunications + Media.

Minimum salary for assignments: $100,000
Retained search
Industries: consumer, healthcare, hospitals, biotechnology, bio-equipment, industrial, non-profits, venture capital/private equity, consulting, management consulting, accounting, hi-tech, communications, telecommunications e-commerce, internet, new media
Positions: most positions, board of directors, senior management, financial, human resources, information technology, MIS, attorneys, paralegals, operations, manufacturing, sales, marketing, planning logistics management, material management, purchasing
www.acertitude.com

2 Wisconsin Circle
Chevy Chase, MD 20815
301-385-7550
Ms. Jessica Tvelia , Principal /JTvelia@acertitude.com

ADAM JAMES INTERNATIONAL

From the website: Adam James International performs senior level executive search assignments for national and multinational companies. We assist our clients in building world class leadership teams by placing highly qualified executives into key leadership roles and advising clients on workflow and recruitment issues and processes. Our clientele span diverse industries and range in size from entrepreneurial and private equity firms to publicly traded and Fortune 500 corporations. These clients retain us to quickly identify and secure senior level executives that improve bottom line performance and fill key leadership needs. We believe that a client relationship rooted in partnership and executed in advisement guarantees long-term customer satisfaction.

Minimum salary for assignments: $100,000
Retained search
Most industries
Positions: most positions, senior management
www.AdamJames.com

1101 Pennsylvania Avenue NW, 3rd Floor
Washington, DC 20004
303-785-7900
Mr. Ken Philbrick , Partner /Ken@AdamJames.com

ADECCO STAFFING

From the website: Adecco USA - Through five integrated business lines, Adecco Group companies in the USA provide a comprehensive range of human resource services, from temporary and full-time staffing to managed and career services, e-business solutions and beyond. Adecco Staffing, the largest staffing and HR solutions company in the world, puts more than 650,000 people to work every day in virtually every field of employment - from clerical to industrial, financial to technical, hospitality to airport, to call center and beyond.

No minimum salary for assignments
Contingency search
Industries: most industries, accounting, banking, construction, engineering, financial services, healthcare, hospitals, hi-tech, hospitality, hotels, restaurants, government, public administration, manufacturing publishing, retail trade, services
Positions: administration, accounting, call centers, engineering, human resources, industrial labor, logistics management, material management, manufacturing, marketing, sales, security, technical, scientific telecommunications, interim, contract, temporary placement
www.adeccousa.com

7939 Honeygo Boulevard, Suite 208
Baltimore, MD 21236
410-931-4009
Ms. Asysha Hogan , Senior Recruiter /Asysha.Hogan@adeccona.com
Ms. Jessica Simons , Client Program Manager /Jessica.Simons@adeccona.com/ /industries GEN/BAN/HEA/MAN/RTL/HIT/positions ADM/ACC/CAL/IND/SAL/TEC
Mr. Matt Webb , Regional Account Director /Matt.Webb@adeccona.com/ /industries GEN/BAN/HEA/MAN/RTL/HIT/positions ADM/ACC/CAL/IND/SAL/TEC
Mr. Justin Pabon , Director of Operations /Justin.Pabon@adeccona.com/ /industries GEN/BAN/HEA/MAN/RTL/HIT/positions ADM/ACC/CAL/IND/SAL/TEC
Ms. Emily Hebert , Director of Strategic Accounts /Emily.Hebert@adeccona.com/ /industries GEN/BAN/HEA/MAN/RTL/HIT/positions ADM/ACC/CAL/IND/SAL/TEC
Ms. Brynn Bagg , Client Account Manager /Brynn.Bagg@adeccona.com/ /industries HEA/positions ADM/ACC/CAL/IND/SAL/TEC

9861 Brokenland Parkway, Suite 105
Columbia, MD 21046

410-290-5803
Mr. Matt Webb , Regional Account Director /Matt.Webb@adeccona.com
Mr. Kernan Kelly , Branch Manager /Kernan.Kelly@adeccona.com/ /industries GEN/GOV/positions MIS/NET/TEL

ADVANTAGE TECHNICAL RESOURCING

From the website: The Advantage of Advantage Resourcing)(r) As one of the world's leading staffing companies, our primary objective is clear-cut: To perfectly align the best people with appropriate positions for our clients everywhere. >> Advantage Technical Resourcing -- Provides Contract, Contract-to-Hire and Permanent Placement Services in the following primary skill set categories: * Project managers * Software developers * IT operations specialists * Mechanical engineers * Construction engineers * Environmental engineers * System engineers * Licensed aerospace engineers * R&D scientists * Inorganic and organic chemists >> Advantage Professional -- Provides Contract, Contract-to-Hire and Permanent Placement Services in the following primary skill set categories: * Accounting & Finance * Banking & Financial Services * Executive Assistants & Business Support * Human Resources * Executive * Legal >> Advantage Staffing -- Provides Contract, Contract-to-Hire and Permanent Placement Services in the following primary skill set categories: * Administrative & Clerical * Skilled Trades * Light Industrial & Manufacturing * Construction * Call Center * Hospitality * Distribution and Logistics * Retail >> Advantage xPO -- Specializes in strategic workforce planning and customized solutions that meet our customers' unique talent acquisition needs.

Minimum salary for assignments: $40,000
Contingency search
Industries: most industries, manufacturing, engineering, hi-tech, software
Positions: engineering, information technology, MIS, networks, LAN, WAN, interim, contract, temporary placement
www.advantageresourcing.com

10632 Little Patuxent Parkway
Columbia, MD 21044
800-888-7864
Mr. Chris Bieneman , Marketing Manager /Chris.Bieneman@advantageresourcing.com
Mr. Brian Meehan , Senior Technical Recruiter /Brian.Meehan@advantageresourcing.com/ /industries GEN/positions ENG/MIS/NET/TEM
Mr. Patrick Meehan , Account Executive /Patrick.Meehan@advantageresourcing.com/ /industries GEN/positions ENG/MIS/NET/TEM
Mr. Harry Torbit , Senior Technical Recruiter /Harry.Torbit@advantageresourcing.com/ /industries GEN/positions ENG/MIS/NET/TEM
Mr. Michael Gray , Senior Account Executive /Michael.Gray@advantageresourcing.com/ /industries GEN/positions ENG/MIS/NET/TEM

ALIXPARTNERS

From the website: AlixPartners is a global firm of senior business and consulting professionals that specializes in improving corporate financial and operational performance, executing corporate turnarounds and providing litigation consulting and forensic accounting services when it really matters - in urgent, high-impact situations. At AlixPartners, we bring a rich heritage of helping companies through the toughest of times. With more than a hundred senior professionals, all with a wide variety of industry and functional experience, we are execution-oriented and implementation-focused, delivering results, not reports. AlixPartners delivers services in the following core practices: * Corporate Turnaround & Restructuring * Enterprise Improvement * Information Management Services * Financial Advisory Services * Litigation Consulting & Corporate Investigations.

Minimum salary for assignments: $100,000
Retained search
Industries: consulting, management consulting
Positions: consulting, interim, contract, temporary placement
www.alixpartners.com

2099 Pennsylvania Avenue NW, Suite 300
Washington, DC 20006
202-756-9000/fax 202-756-9300
Ms. Susan Markel , Managing Director /SMarkel@alixpartners.com
Ms. Angela Zutavern , Managing Director /AZutavern@alixpartners.com/ /industries CSG/positions CNS/TEM
Mr. Tom Antisdel , Managing Director /TAntisdel@alixpartners.com/ /industries CSG/positions CNS/TEM

APOLLO PROFESSIONAL SOLUTIONS, INC.

From the website: Apollo began as a regional supplier providing Engineering and Information Technology staffing services to companies throughout New England and has emerged a national supplier providing these services in 42 states. A premier provider of Engineering, Information Technology and Professional Staffing services. Apollo is committed to providing the highest level of quality customer service and ethical standards to the business of contract, and direct placement staffing services. Specialties: Contract and temporary staffing for Engineering and Technical industry.

Minimum salary for assignments: $40,000
Contingency search
Industries: most industries, industrial, manufacturing
Positions: engineering, information technology, MIS, networks, LAN, WAN, interim, contract, temporary placement
www.apollopros.com

7310 Ritchie Highway. Suite 400
Glen Burnie, MD 21061
443-891-0440/fax 410-768-7888
Ms. Eileen Crawford , Southeast Regional Manager /ECrawford@apollopros.com
Mr. Jim Pyle , Technical Recruiter /JPyle@apollopros.com/ /industries GEN/IND/MAN/positions ENG/MIS/NET/TEM

Ms. Monica Berron , Technical Recruiter /MBerron@apollopros.com/ /industries GEN/IND/MAN/positions ENG/MIS/NET/TEM

AQUENT

From the website: Aquent is a professional services firm that specializes in helping companies all over the world, across a variety of industries, make use of people, processes, and technology more effectively than ever before. Since its founding in 1986, Aquent's pioneering approach to staffing, consulting, and outsourcing keeps the company a step ahead. Among its many industry-leading innovations, Aquent was the first company in the United States to offer comprehensive benefits to temporary employees, including a company-matching 401(k) plan. In addition, Aquent was the first in the field to offer an unconditional 110% money-back guarantee to clients, and the first to create a Web site featuring thousands of portfolios created by prequalified talent. We also offer a range of outsourcing and technical solutions aimed at improving the efficiency of marketing execution.

Minimum salary for assignments: $40,000
Contingency search
Industries: most industries, communications, telecommunications, consulting, management consulting, information technology, computer services, data processing, entertainment, film, gaming, hi-tech, software wireless communications, e-commerce, internet, new media
Positions: call centers, graphic arts, graphic design, information technology, MIS, networks, LAN, WAN, interim, contract, temporary placement
www.aquent.com

8 Market Place, Suite 300
Baltimore, MD 21202
410-332-1833/fax 877-730-9078
Ms. Cynthia Escalante , Talent Management Lead /CEscalante@aquent.com
Ms. Lee Andrese , Vice President /LAndrese@aquent.com/ /industries GOV/positions CAL/GRA/MIS/NET/TEM

1025 Connecticut Avenue NW, Suite 901
Washington, DC 20036
202-293-5700
Ms. Michelle Oldham , Managing Director /MOldham@aquent.com
Ms. Tina Tozzi , Director, Strategic Accounts /TTozzi@aquent.com/ /industries NP/positions ADV/CAL/GRA/MIS/NET/TEM
Mr. Ray Thurman , Director, Government Sector /RThurman@aquent.com/ /industries GOV/positions ADV/CAL/GRA/MIS/NET/TEM
Mr. Christopher Woodbridge , Agent /CWoodbridge@aquent.com/ /industries GEN/ADV/FIN/ENT/SFT/WWW/positions ADV/CAL/GRA/MAR/TEM
Ms. Alyssa O'Keefe , Agent /AOKeefe@aquent.com/ /industries GEN/ADV/FIN/ENT/SFT/WWW/positions ADV/CAL/GRA/MIS/NET/TEM

ASSIGNED COUNSEL INCORPORATED

From the website: Assigned Counsel provides legal staffing services to corporation law departments, law firms, government agencies and nonprofit organizations with attorneys on a temporary or temp-to-hire basis. Whether you need help for a day, a month, a year or indefinitely, Assigned Counsel can help you hand-pick the right person for the job. You tell us the specialty you require - and we'll deliver exactly what you need. Our clients consistently praise us for providing attorneys whose quality and fit match their needs. We created the first quality management program in our industry. Survey results show 97.7% of Assigned Counsel placed attorneys meet or exceed clients' expectations.

Minimum salary for assignments: $100,000
Contingency search
Industries: most industries, law firms, government, public administration, non-profits
Positions: attorneys, paralegals, interim, contract, temporary placement
www.assignedcounsel.com

6701 Democracy Boulevard, Suite 300
Bethesda, MD 20817
301-571-9322
Ms. Alisa Austin, Esq. , Senior Recruiting Attorney /AAustin@assignedcounsel.com
Ms. Jill Boggs , Business Development Manager /JBoggs@assignedcounsel.com/ /industries GEN/LAW/GOV/NP/positions LAW/TEM

BBSI

From the website: Barrett Business Services launched as a temporary staffing service in 1951, and has since been at the forefront of the industry by developing and providing innovative staffing services to thousands of companies across the United States. The industry has evolved from simply being suppliers of "temporary" workers in mostly unskilled or lower-skilled classifications on short-term assignments. We work diligently to educate our customers on how to use our range of services to their best advantage. We guide them through issues involving how to staff for variable production cycles due to seasonality or unexpected increases in customer demand or long-term projects. The efficiencies and economies of "just-in-time" staffing has made this concept a standard practice for many companies. We continue to experience a demand for the traditional types of replacement or supplemental staff needed to handle short-term assignments to cover for an employee out on vacation, seasonal shifts in business or Family Medical Leave, as a few examples. We've become very proficient in helping our clients fill the following positions: Secretaries * Word Processors * Receptionists * General Office * Clerks * Switchboard Operators * Data Entry * Collators * Demonstrators * Expeditors * Telemarketers * Customer Service * Trade Show Staff * Accounts Payable * Payroll Clerks * Bookkeepers * Administrative Assistants * Document Control * Computer When you partner with the industrial division of Barrett, you're working with a leader in providing qualified skilled people for your job assignment. We pride ourselves on finding the right person the first time, every time. Every person is thoroughly screened to make sure we have a perfect match. Whether you're looking for inventory control people, drivers, warehouse workers, or production assemblers, we have systems in place that can retrieve exact matches based on job related skills, education or work experience.

Minimum salary for assignments: $30,000
Contingency search
Industries: most industries
Positions: accounting, administration, drivers, human resources, industrial labor, manufacturing,

medical, physicians, nurses, therapists, information technology, MIS, interim, contract, temporary placement
www.barrettbusiness.com

4940 Campbell Boulevard, Suite 250
Baltimore, MD 21236
410-583-7711/fax 410-583-0018
Ms. Jean Gallo , Area Manager /Towson-MD_Jobs@bbsihq.com
Mr. Jonathan Patkus , Business Development Manager /Jonathan.Patkus@bbsihq.com/ /industries GEN/positions ACC/ADM/HRS/IND/MAN/MIS
Ms. Nancy O'Neill , Business Development Manager /Nancy.ONeill@bbsihq.com/ /industries GEN/positions ACC/ADM/HRS/IND/MAN/MIS
Mr. Kevin Via , Client Business Partner /Kevin.Via@bbsihq.com/ /industries GEN/positions ACC/ADM/HRS/IND/MAN/MIS

220 East Main Street, Suite A
Salisbury, MD 21801
410-546-2020/fax 410-546-8403
Mr. Tony Nichols , Area Manager /Salisbury-MD_Jobs@bbsihq.com

---

BCG ATTORNEY SEARCH

From the website: Welcome to BCG Attorney Search -- a legal recruitment firm that has built its reputation on maintaining high standards across the board. BCG Attorney Search is the most selective legal staffing firm in the US, providing clients with a level of service that's second to none. With over a decade of experience, BCG Attorney Search averages more than one placement a day.

Minimum salary for assignments: $75,000
Contingency search
Industries: most industries, law firms
Positions: attorneys, paralegals
www.bcgsearch.com

1629 K Street NW
Washington, DC 20006
202-955-5585
Ms. Nadeen Weybrecht , Legal Recruiter /NadeenW@bcgsearch.com

---

BATTALIA WINSTON

rom the website: Battalia Winston is an executive search firm that has been helping companies -- from early stage to Fortune 100 companies -- find and retain top executives for more than 50 years. As a mid-sized executive search firm with global reach, Battalia Winston is a better fit for companies looking to secure the best executive talent for their organizations. Through our customized candidate research, in-depth competitive analysis and hands on partner search process, Battalia Winston helps ensure that our clients attract the executives they need today to achieve their strategic goals. Located in major markets nationwide, our executive recruiters develop industry-specific, results-driven talent acquisition solutions. We identify executives whose backgrounds, skill sets and values align with our clients' strategic vision and unique company culture.

Minimum salary for assignments: $150,000
Retainer/AESC or MAJOR
Industries: most industries, law firms, broadcasting, media, TV, radio, cable TV, entertainment, film, gaming, hi-tech, services, consulting, management consulting, accounting
Positions: most positions, accounting, consulting, development, fund raising, engineering, financial, human resources, manufacturing, marketing, information technology, MIS, , sales, technical, scientific, senior management
www.battaliawinston.com

1015 15th Street NW
Washington, DC 20005
202-626-8080
Ms. Dale Winston , Chairwoman & CEO /DWinston@battaliawinston.com

---

BEACON HILL STAFFING GROUP

From the website: Beacon Hill Staffing Group was founded to set a new standard in search, career placement and flexible staffing. Our niche brands provide direct hire, executive search, temporary staffing, contract consulting and temp/contract-to-hire solutions to emerging growth companies and the Fortune 500 across market sectors, career specialties/disciplines and industries. Over time, office locations, specialty practice areas and service offerings will be added to address ever changing constituent needs. Learn more about Beacon Hill Staffing Group and our specialty divisions, Beacon Hill Associates, Beacon Hill Financial, Beacon Hill HR, Beacon Hill Government Services, Beacon Hill Legal, Beacon Hill Pharma and Beacon Hill Technologies by visiting www.beaconhillstaffing.com.

Minimum salary for assignments: $40,000
Contingency search
Industries: most industries, banking, financial services, law firms, government, public administration, healthcare, hospitals
Positions: accounting, auditing, financial, taxes, risk management, interim, contract, temporary placement
www.beaconhillstaffing.com

9211 Corporate Boulevard
Rockville, MD 20850
240-715-0360/fax 240-715-0379
Ms. Jana Chehayeb , Senior Staffing Consultant /JChehayeb@beaconhillsg.com
Mr. Steve Broadman , Division Director, Government Technology /SBroadman@beaconhillsg.com/ /industries GOV/positions MIS/NET/TEL
Ms. Alyssa Axthelm , IT Staffing Consultant /AAxthelm@beaconhillsg.com/ /industries GEN/BAN/FIN/LAW/GOV/HEA/positions MIS/NET/TEM
Ms. Allie Solomon , Financial Staffing Consultant /ASolomon@beaconhillsg.com/ /industries GEN/BAN/FIN/LAW/GOV/HEA/positions ACC/AUD/FIN/TAX/CRE/CAS

Ms. Kim Ayers , Market Director /KAyers@beaconhillsg.com/ /industries GEN/BAN/FIN/LAW/GOV/HEA/positions ACC/AUD/FIN/TAX/RIS/MIS
Mr. Mitch Trestrail , Technical Recruiter /MTrestrail@beaconhillsg.com/ /industries GOV/SEC/positions SEC/MIS
Mr. Benjamin Flint , Staffing Consultant /BFlint@beaconhillsg.com/ /industries GEN/BAN/FIN/LAW/GOV/HEA/positions ACC/AUD/FIN/TAX/RIS/CRE

1120 Connecticut Avenue NW, Suite 480
Washington, DC 20036
202-393-6600/fax 202-393-6767
Ms. Kristen Johnson , Division Director /KJohnson@beaconhillsg.com
Ms. Kendall Smardzewski , Division Director, Legal /KSmardzewski@beaconhillsg.com/ /industries GEN/BAN/FIN/LAW/GOV/HEA/positions LAW/TEM
Ms. Jen Daisey , Senior Staffing Consultant /JDaisey@beaconhillsg.com/ /industries GEN/BAN/FIN/LAW/GOV/HEA/positions ADM/ACC/FIN/HRS/LAW/MIS
Mr. Christopher Rimorin , Director /CRimorin@beaconhillsg.com/ /industries GEN/BAN/FIN/LAW/GOV/HEA/positions ADM/ACC/FIN/HRS/LAW/MIS
Ms. Maja Bijelic , Senior Staffing Consultant /MBijelic@beaconhillsg.com/ /industries GEN/BAN/FIN/LAW/GOV/HEA/positions ADM/ACC/FIN/HRS/LAW/MIS
Ms. Mia Eckstein , Business Development Manager /MEckstein@beaconhillsg.com/ /industries GEN/BAN/FIN/LAW/GOV/HEA/positions MIS/NET/TEM
Ms. Yinka Morakinyo , Account Executive /YMorakinyo@beaconhillsg.com/ /industries GEN/BAN/FIN/LAW/GOV/HEA/positions ADM/ACC/FIN/HRS/LAW/MIS

BECKETT MCLAUGHLIN INTERNATIONAL, LLC

From the website: Beckett McLaughlin International, LLC (BMI) is a full-service Global Executive Recruiting firm that is well positioned to provide successful solutions for the rapidly increasing global competition to locate and acquire the best-qualified talent. As companies strive to become more competitive, change is inevitable. Whether brought on by rapid growth, a public offering or competitive initiatives, major changes continually challenge an organization's ability to be competitive and respond appropriately.

Minimum salary for assignments: $100,000
Retained search
Industries: most industries, banking, real estate, construction, energy, government, public administration, hospitality, hotels, restaurants, insurance, investment banks, merchant banks, biotechnology, bio-equipment, manufacturing non-profits, accounting, security services and products
Positions: most positions, accounting, financial, human resources, information technology, MIS, auditing, engineering, security, sales, marketing, planning, logistics management, material management, purchasing, international
www.bmrintl.com

877 Baltimore Annapolis Boulevard, Suite 310
Severna Park, MD 21146
410-975-9622/fax 410-432-6107
Mr. Richard Beckett , Managing Partner /RBeckett@bmrintl.com
Ms. Lisa Tucker , Executive Vice President /LTucker@bmrintl.com/ /generalist

Ms. Ashleigh Diefenderfer, Manager of Recruiting & Administration /Ashleigh@bmrintl.com/
/generalist

BELCAN

From the website: Belcan Corporation provides engineering, staffing, and other flexible workforce solutions to clients around the globe. A dedication to the success of our clients and employees, along with a commitment to a core set of beliefs that start with integrity, has led to over 50 years of growth and success. From jet engines to electronics, heavy equipment to pharmaceuticals, and distribution centers to manufacturing, Belcan takes a partnering approach to provide customer-driven solutions that are flexible, scalable, and cost-effective.

Minimum salary for assignments: $75,000
Contingency search
Industries: most industries, aerospace, biotechnology, bio-equipment, chemicals, communications, telecommunications, construction, defense, transportation, pharmaceuticals, drugs, biologicals, automotive, motor vehicles, trucks information technology, computer services, data processing, equipment, machinery, industrial,
Positions: automation, design, engineering, information technology, MIS, manufacturing, project management, quality, interim, contract, temporary placement
www.belcan.com

101 Lakeforest Boulevard
Gaithersburg, MD 20877
301-921-8811
Mr. Brian Deming, Vice President, Recruiting /BDeming@belcan.com
Mr. Lee Shabe, President of Belcan Government Services /LShabe@belcan.com/ /industries GOV/DEF/positions AUT/DES/ENG/MAN/MIS/QUA
Ms. Christina Adams, Client Executive /CAdams@belcan.com/ /industries GEN/CMM/DEF/PHR/IND/ENR/positions AUT/DES/ENG/MAN/MIS/QUA
Mr. Tim Cross, Senior Technical Recruiter /TCross@belcan.com/ /industries GEN/CMM/DEF/PHR/IND/ENR/positions AUT/DES/ENG/MAN/MIS/QUA
Ms. Haily Nguyen, Director of Marketing and Communications /HNguyen@belcan.com/ /industries GEN/CMM/DEF/PHR/IND/ENR/positions AUT/DES/ENG/MAN/MIS/QUA

CORESTAFF SERVICES

From the website: CORESTAFF Services is focused on potential. Our goal is to create opportunities for talented people to excel and strategies to help companies grow and prosper. CORESTAFF provides staffing, human resources solutions, outsourcing, and consulting services for Accounting & Finance, Administrative & Clerical, Call Center, Customer Care, Clinical Research & Scientific, Engineering, Information Management, Information Technology, Light Industrial & Assembly, and Professional skills sets. CORESTAFF maintains a local presence through a powerful, connected regional center and branch network across the United States, including InfoCurrent, Leafstone, s.com and SRG Woolf, and is ranked among the 50 largest staffing services organizations in the U.S. CORESTAFF is a wholly owned subsidiary of Impellam Group, plc.

Minimum salary for assignments: $40,000
Contingency search
Industries: most industries, communications, telecommunications, software, computers, wireless communications, e-commerce, internet, new media
Positions: most positions, accounting, financial, administration, call centers, human resources, information technology, MIS, industrial labor, interim, contract, temporary placement
www.corestaff.com

12300 Twinbrook Parkway, Suite 210
Rockville, MD 20852
301-949-9444
Ms. Renee Norman , Area Sales Director /Renee.Norman@corestaff.com
Mr. Darnell Morris , Staffing Specialist /Darnell.Morris@corestaff.com/ /industries GEN/CMM/SFT/CMP/WIR/WWW/positions ACC/ENG/HRS/MIS/MAR/SAL
Mr. Robert Ford , Area Sales Director /Robert.Ford@corestaff.com/ /industries CMM/SFT/CMP/WIR/WWW/positions ACC/ENG/HRS/MIS/MAR/SAL
Mr. Matt Grimes , Technical Recruiter /Matt.Grimes@corestaff.com/ /industries GEN/CMM/SFT/CMP/WIR/WWW/positions ACC/ENG/HRS/MIS/MAR/SAL
Mr. Mike Guilday , Practice Director /Mike.Guilday@corestaff.com/ /industries HIT/ENG/CMM/WIR/positions MIS/NET/TEL
Ms. Jan Morgan , Branch Service Manager /Jan.Morgan@corestaff.com/ /industries GEN/CMM/SFT/CMP/WIR/WWW/positions ACC/ENG/HRS/MIS/MAR/SAL
Ms. Diane Ribera , Client Solutions Manager /Diane.Ribera@corestaff.com/ /industries GEN/CMM/SFT/CMP/WIR/WWW/positions ACC/ENG/HRS/MIS/MAR/SAL

900 17th Street NW, Suite 310
Washington, DC 20006
202-223-4900
Ms. Jan Morgan , Branch Service Manager /WashingtonDC@corestaff.com

---

CSI EXECUTIVE SEARCH

From the website: From resource ... through relationship ... to the end point of best results, CSI Executive Search is your partner for Pinpoint Placements . Whether you need to fill a single mission critical position or multiple positions in a broader industry niche, our 10 years of vertical integration in the accounting, engineering, health care, information technology, legal, and operations arenas position us to be your go-to people solution. Specialties: executive search, accounting, finance, engineering, information technology, legal, marketing, manufacturing, operational, supply chain/logistics, medical device, oil/gas, energy, IT, renewable energy

Minimum salary for assignments: $100,000
Retainer/AESC or MAJOR
Industries: construction, consumer, environmental, green industries, healthcare, hospitals, information technology, computer services, data processing, manufacturing, , venture capital/private equity transportation
Positions: accounting, financial, marketing, engineering, medical, physicians, nurses, therapists, human resources, attorneys, paralegals, manufacturing, operations, logistics management, material management
www.csi-executivesearch.com

2200 Pennsylvania Avenue NW
Washington, DC 20037
877-329-1825
Mr. Asa Sphar, PhD , Vice President /info@csi-executivesearch.com

---

CENTERSTONE EXECUTIVE SEARCH & CONSULTING

From the website: Centerstone Executive Search & Consulting is a specialty boutique firm that consistently delivers excellence in executive search services at the Board Director and C-Suite level, contemporary leadership and organizational consulting solutions, and a range of board services to new ventures to Fortune 500 companies. With offices in Washington DC, New York, Philadelphia, Charleston, Seattle and Los Angeles, we are a national retained firm that strategically partners with clients to ensure expert composition, selection and development of their Board and C-Suite leadership teams. We invest in close client relationships, with a market portfolio that spans consumer products and services across retail, digital/eCommerce, wholesale, hospitality and retail healthcare, as well as federal contracting in aerospace, defense and security.

Minimum salary for assignments: $150,000
Retained search
Industries: consumer, retail trade, wholesale trade, e-commerce, internet, new media, hospitality, hotels, restaurants, healthcare, hospitals, direct marketing
Positions: most positions, accounting, advertising, financial, human resources, marketing, information technology, MIS, sales, senior management
www.centerstonesearch.com

2200 Pennsylvania Ave NW, 4th Floor
Washington, DC 20037
202-847-4867
Mr. Jim Donnelly , Managing Director /Jim@centerstonesearch.com
Ms. Lauren Trombetta , Manager, Client and Candidate Services /Lauren@centerstonesearch.com/ /industries CON/RTL/WWW/HSP/HEA/DIR/positions GEN/ACC/ADV/FIN/HRS/MAR
Mr. Andrew Rahaman , Associate Consultant /Andrew@centerstonesearch.com/ /industries CON/RTL/WWW/HSP/HEA/DIR/positions GEN/ACC/ADV/FIN/HRS/MAR

COLUMBIA CONSULTING GROUP, INC.

From the website: Columbia Consulting Group has nearly 30 years experience finding the qualified executives to seize the challenges of today and the opportunities of tomorrow. We bring to the search process the same sense of urgency which our clients possess in meeting their business objectives. Even though we are a generalist search firm, the following industry practice areas are where we have extensive recruitment expertise: * Financial Services * Manufacturing * German, Austrian, Swiss Subsidiaries * Technology * Healthcare * Private Equity * Association and Non-Profit * Infrastructure * Financial Executives.

Minimum salary for assignments: $125,000
Retainer/AESC or MAJOR
Industries: most industries, financial services, manufacturing, hi-tech, healthcare, hospitals, venture capital/private equity, non-profits, construction
Positions: most positions, financial, human resources, manufacturing, marketing, medical, physicians, nurses, therapists, , sales, senior management, technical, scientific
www.ccgsearch.com

5525 Twin Knolls Road
Columbia, MD 21045
443-276-2525/fax 443-276-2536
Mr. Lawrence Holmes , Managing Director /LHolmes@ccgsearch.com
Mr. Matthew Kostmayer , Managing Director /MKostmayer@ccgsearch.com/ /industries FIN/INS/positions GEN/FIN/HRS/MAN/MAR/SEN
Mr. Corey Holmes , Managing Director /CHolmes@ccgsearch.com/ /industries FIN/HEA/MAN/CMM/CON/positions GEN/FIN/HRS/MAN/MAR/SEN
Mr. James King , Managing Director /JKing@ccgsearch.com/ /industries FIN/HEA/HIT/MAN/ENR/positions GEN/FIN/HRS/MAN/MAR/SEN
Mr. Thomas McMahon , Managing Director /TMcMahon@ccgsearch.com/ /industries FIN/HEA/INS/MAN/positions GEN/FIN/HRS/MAN/MAR/SEN

COMPUTER ENTERPRISES, INC.

From the website: Computer Enterprises, Inc. -- Since its founding in 1992, CEI has delivered high quality software development solutions to companies of all sizes. Our architects use their experience to deliver complex projects that solve real business problems. CEI strives to be a thought leader in Microsoft, Java, Open Source and Mobile development. We are an IT focused company. Our Staff Supplementation services utilize our proprietary Exact Match(tm) process reducing unnecessary interviews and ensuring a faster time to fill. 20 years of experience and 1000's of successful consultant engagements have taught us that quality is all important in this industry. Our unyielding commitment to quality has ensured our success and longevity and has allowed us to work with companies both large and small including over 60% of the Fortune 50.

Minimum salary for assignments: $50,000
Contingency search
Industries: most industries, energy, utilities, healthcare, hospitals, law firms, e-commerce, internet, new media, financial services, industrial, manufacturing, transportation, software, communications, telecommunications government, public administration
Positions: information technology, MIS, networks, LAN, WAN, interim, contract, temporary placement
www.ceiamerica.com

901 K Street NW, Suite 300
Washington, DC 20001
412-341-3541
Mr. Joseph Lavezzo , Director of Operations, DC /JLavezzo@ceiamerica.com
Mr. Christopher Wootten , Senior Solutions Account Executive /CWootten@ceiamerica.com/ /industries GEN/ENR/HEA/WWW/FIN/MAN/positions MIS/NET/TEM

CREATIVE CIRCLE

*From the website: Creative Circle is a specialized staffing agency that connects innovative advertising, marketing, creative, and interactive professionals with companies seeking talent on a full-time or freelance basis. Account Planners or Account Strategists * Information Architects * Content Strategists * Copywriters * Interactive Art Directors or Designers * Front End Web Developers and Back End Web Developers * Graphic Designers * Print Producers * Art Directors * Creative Directors * Producers * Presentation Designers.*

Minimum salary for assignments: $25,000
Contingency search
Industries: most industries, advertising, public relations, entertainment, film, gaming, e-commerce, internet, new media
Positions: advertising, graphic arts, graphic design, marketing, information technology, MIS, interim, contract, temporary placement
www.creativecircle.com

1130 Connecticut Ave NW, Suite 650
Washington, DC 20036
202-827-2207/fax 888-856-7677
Ms. Bailey O'Connell , Senior Recruiter /BOConnell@creativecircle.com
Ms. Teresa Schefer , Senior Recruiter /TSchefer@creativecircle.com/ /industries GEN/ADV/ENT/WWW/positions ADV/GRA/MAR/MIS/TEM
Ms. Meghan C. Hinder , Recruiter /MCashen@creativecircle.com/ /industries GEN/ADV/ENT/WWW/positions ADV/GRA/MAR/MIS/TEM
Ms. Amanda Cavanaugh , Account Executive /ACavanaugh@creativecircle.com/ /industries GEN/ADV/ENT/WWW/positions ADV/GRA/MAR/MIS/TEM
Ms. Tiffany Green , Account Executive /TGreen@creativecircle.com/ /industries GEN/ADV/ENT/WWW/positions ADV/GRA/MAR/MIS/TEM
Ms. Hannah Buck , Recruiter /HBuck@creativecircle.com/ /industries GEN/ADV/ENT/WWW/positions ADV/GRA/MAR/MIS/TEM
Mr. Dalan Carter , Creative Recruiter /DCarter@creativecircle.com/ /industries GEN/ADV/ENT/WWW/positions ADV/GRA/MAR/MIS/TEM

THE CREATIVE GROUP

From the website: The Creative Group provides a comprehensive range of freelance creative, advertising, marketing and Internet professionals to a variety of companies. The Creative Group, a division of specialized staffing leader Robert Half International Inc., focuses on placing freelance professionals in the creative, advertising, marketing, web and public relations fields. As companies develop short- and long-term strategies for building visibility in an increasingly competitive marketplace, they require immediate access to specialized freelancers. As more and more firms look to supplement their in-house creative and communications teams and outsource projects, they look to The Creative Group for consultants who possess expertise in a range of areas, including Internet design, direct marketing, e-marketing and media relations.

Minimum salary for assignments: $30,000

Contingency search
Industries: most industries, advertising, public relations, communications, telecommunications, computers, construction, financial services, food and beverages, healthcare, hospitals, manufacturing, services software, wholesale trade, e-commerce, internet, new media, transportation
Positions: advertising, graphic arts, graphic design, marketing, information technology, MIS, public relations, interim, contract, temporary placement
www.creativegroup.com

1401 Eye Street NW, 4th Floor
Washington, DC 20005
202-626-0290/fax 202-626-4950
Ms. Kristen Herberg , Vice President /washington.dc@creativegroup.com
Ms. Lauren Dobos , Vice President & Division Director /Lauren.Dobos@creativegroup.com/ /industries GEN/ADV/WWW/FIN/MAN/SER/positions ADV/GRA/MAR/MIS/PRE/TEM
Ms. Paula Morrison , Recruiting Manager /Paula.Morrison@creativegroup.com/ /industries GEN/ADV/WWW/FIN/MAN/SER/positions ADV/GRA/MAR/MIS/PRE
Ms. Diana Vanderbei , Senior Digital Recruiter /Diana.Vanderbei@creativegroup.com/ /industries GEN/ADV/WWW/FIN/MAN/SER/positions ADV/GRA/MAR/MIS/PRE
Ms. Linda Nguyen , Account Manager /Linda.Nguyen@creativegroup.com/ /industries GEN/ADV/WWW/FIN/MAN/SER/positions ADV/GRA/MAR/MIS/PRE/TEM
Ms. Diana Vanderbei , Creative Recruiter /Diana.Vanderbei@creativegroup.com/ /industries GEN/ADV/WWW/FIN/MAN/SER/positions ADV/GRA/MAR/MIS/PRE/TEM
Ms. Janet Baptiste , Account Executive /Janet.Baptiste@creativegroup.com/ /industries GEN/ADV/WWW/FIN/MAN/SER/positions ADV/GRA/MAR/MIS/PRE

CROSS HILL PARTNERS, LLC

From the website: Cross Hill Partners, LLC -- We are not your typical search firm. As a boutique firm, we are very discriminating in the work we take on. If we partner with a client on an assignment, it is because we want to, not because we are required to by broader company objectives. As a result, in representing our clients and engagements to the market, we do so with heartfelt commitment and enthusiasm. We have flexibility in structuring terms of an engagement and we do all work ourselves. You know who is doing the heavy lifting, and it's either Diane or Chris. Our client roster includes national and international institutions of higher education, academic medicine, cultural and advocacy organizations, and corporations. We invite you to visit our website to learn more about our process, our partners and our experience.

Minimum salary for assignments: $150,000
Retained search
Industries: education, higher education, non-profits, healthcare, hospitals
Positions: most positions, development, fund raising, senior management, information technology, MIS, sales, marketing, financial
www.crosshillpartners.com

1725 I Street NW
Washington, DC 20006
202-380-9331
Mr. Christopher Shea , Managing Partner /CShea@crosshillpartners.com

Ms. Diane Shea , Managing Partner /DShea@crosshillpartners.com/ /industries ED/NP/HEA/positions GEN/DEV/MIS/SAL/MAR/FIN

CROWN ADVISORS, INC.

From the website: Crown Advisors focuses exclusively on providing executive search consulting services for clients in the real estate industry. Crown serves clients covering the full spectrum of real estate activities, including REITs and public corporations, developers, homebuilders, property managers, institutional investors, investment banks and lenders, funds and advisors, architects and appraisers, construction companies and engineering firms, among others.

Minimum salary for assignments: $100,000
Retained search
Industries: construction, real estate
Positions: most positions, accounting, financial, marketing, senior management
www.crownsearch.com

Washington, DC
202-400-2948
Ms. Kimball Wood , Partner /Kimball@crownsearch.com

CURTIS HALL PARTNERS

From the website: Curtis Hall Partners -- Curtis Hall Partners is a retainer-based executive search firm comprised of search professionals, human capital subject matter experts, industry executives and thought leaders in a variety of industries, including healthcare, technology and financial services. For more than 20 years, our partners have established an exemplary record of providing advice and identifying and recruiting outstanding executives to our client firms.

Minimum salary for assignments: $100,000
Retained search
Industries: healthcare, hospitals, biotechnology, bio-equipment, financial services, hi-tech
Positions: senior management, financial, information technology, MIS, marketing, sales
www.curtishallpartners.com

327 Warren Avenue
Baltimore, MD 21230
443-253-4383/fax 410-814-3224
Mr. Philip Grantham , Principal /PGrantham@curtishallpartners.com
Ms. Lise Perunovich , Principal /LPerunovich@curtishallpartners.com/ /industries HEA/BIO/FIN/HIT/positions SEN/FIN/MIS/MAR/SAL
Mr. Dan Perunovich , Principal /DPerunovich@curtishallpartners.com/ /industries HEA/BIO/FIN/HIT/positions SEN/FIN/MIS/MAR/SAL

DHR INTERNATIONAL

From the website: Established in 1989, DHR is the fifth largest retained executive search firm in the U.S. Since that time, DHR has grown significantly with more than fifty offices worldwide. We conduct search assignments at the Board Director, C-level and functional Vice President levels. Our consultants are experienced professionals who are retained by Fortune 1000 as well as prominent venture firms and early-stage companies. Since inception, DHR has been guided by its founding principles. Foremost, the consultants of DHR hold the highest of ethical standards, along with an unsurpassable level of personal service, an unmatched dedication to quality, and a unique 'value-add' approach. This philosophy and methodology are consistently demonstrated in DHR's thorough and unparalleled researching capability, the full utilization of firm resources on every project, and the timeliness with which we complete our assignments. We feel it is our purpose to be a value-add search firm. We measure our own success based on the success of the leaders and talent we bring to your organization. DHR International provides clients with comprehensive expertise to complete each search successfully. Our practice groups are comprised of experts who possess significant industry knowledge and key relationships. These unique capabilities enable us to meet clients' needs quickly and effectively. Coupled with strong internal collaboration and original research, we approach each search with the best tools and intelligence possible. Practice Groups -- Advanced Technology * Board & CEO * CFO * Consumer * Diversity * Education * Financial Services * Healthcare * Industrial * Life Science * Media & Entertainment * Nonprofit * Professional Services * Retail * Sports * Venture Capital & Private Equity.

Minimum salary for assignments: $125,000
Retainer/AESC or MAJOR
Industries: most industries, hi-tech, consumer, financial services, industrial, automotive, motor vehicles, trucks, venture capital/private equity
Positions: most positions, diversity, multicultural, affirmative action, board of directors, engineering, financial, venture capital, international, manufacturing, marketing, information technology, MIS, purchasing, senior management, technical, scientific
www.dhrinternational.com

900 17th Street NW
Washington, DC 20006
202-774-9366/fax 202-237-0111
Mr. Stephen Hayes , Executive Chairman /SHayes@dhrinternational.com
Ms. Linda Madrid , Executive Vice President /LMadrid@dhrinternational.com/ /industries LAW/REA/FIN/positions LAW/REG
Ms. Julia Eakes , Partner /JEakes@dhrinternational.com/ /industries CON/RTL/positions GEN/FIN/SEN
Mr. Dan Carney , Executive Chairman /DCarney@dhrinternational.com/ /industries HEA/positions GEN/VEN/MIS/TEC/SEN
Mr. Peter Metzger , Vice Chairman /PMetzger@dhrinternational.com/ /industries HIT/SEC/SER/LAW/GOV/NP/positions GEN/LAW/RIS/SEN
Mr. Joe Huddle , Partner /JHuddle@dhrinternational.com/ /industries IND/MAN/TRN/SER/VEN/positions GEN/ENG/IND/MAN/OPS/SEN
Mr. Eugene Patrone , Director /EPatrone@dhrinternational.com/ /industries HIT/GOV/SEC/positions GEN/SEC/MIS/BOD/SEN

DIVERSIFIED SEARCH

From the website: Diversified Search Companies is a generalist retained executive search firm recruiting senior-level management with expertise in a wide range of industries. The firm employs 30 executive recruiters based in Philadelphia, New York, and Boston. We offer industry specialization in Consumer & Industrial; Education, Not-For-Profit, Arts & Culture; Financial & Professional Services; Healthcare & Human Services; Life Sciences; Media & Entertainment; Private Equity; Retail; and Technology. We offer specialization in the functional areas of Board of Directors; Diversity; Chief Financial Officers; Human Resources; Procurement & Supply Chain; and Development & Fundraising.

Minimum salary for assignments: $125,000
Retainer/AESC or MAJOR
Industries: most industries, consumer, retail trade, education, higher education, non-profits, financial services, healthcare, hospitals, industrial, biotechnology, bio-equipment, pharmaceuticals, drugs, biologicals, sports broadcasting, media, TV, radio, cable TV, entertainment, film, gaming, hi-tech
Positions: most positions, board of directors, development, fund raising, financial, human resources, logistics management, material management, purchasing, engineering, information technology, MIS, diversity, multicultural, affirmative action
www.diversifiedsearch.com

1200 New Hampshire Avenue NW
Washington, DC 20036
202-296-2122
Mr. Jason LeÓn , Managing Director /Jason.Leon@divsearch.com
Mr. Dale Jones , Chief Executive Officer /Dale.Jones@divsearch.com/ /industries GEN/CON/ED/NP/positions GEN/BOD/FIN
Ms. Edie Fraser , CEO of STEMconnector /Edie.Fraser@divsearch.com/ /industries GEN/positions ENG/MIS/TEC/AFF/BOD
Ms. Nalini Perkins , Managing Director /Nalini.Perkins@divsearch.com/ /industries ED/NP/HEA/positions GEN/AFF/SEN
Mr. Lionel Anderson , Managing Director /Lionel.Anderson@divsearch.com/ /industries FIN/HEA/HIT/CMM/positions GEN/MIS
Ms. Denielle Pemberton-Heard , General Counsel and Managing Directo /DPembertonHeard@divsearch.com/ /industries CON/RTL/BRO/ENT/SPO/NP/positions GEN/BOD/MAR/DEV/FIN/HRS
Mr. Gene Head , Managing Director /Gene.Head@divsearch.com/ /industries ED/NP/positions GEN/DEV/FIN/HRS/SEN/BOD

EGON ZEHNDER

*From the website: Egon Zehnder has been a force in Executive Search for five decades. We know where to find the executives you need and how to attract the very best talent to your organization. > Functional Practices: * Financial Officers * Human Resources * Information Technology Officers * Legal Professionals * Chief Marketing Officers * Supply Chain * Sustainability. > Industries and Segment: >> Financial Services: Asset Management * Retail Financial Services * Investment Banking, Corporate Banking & Markets * Insurance * Wealth Management * Risk Management * Financial Tech * Infrastructure * Private Equity * Sovereign Wealth Funds >> Technology and Communications: Telecommunications * Digital * Systems, Services and Software * Semiconductors * Fntelligent Systems * Mobile Devices & Apps * Cyber Security * Big Data >> Life Sciences and Healthcare Services Pharmaceuticals * Biotechnology ***

*Generics * Medical Devices * Diagnostics * Healthcare Services * Digital Health * Consumer Health >> Consumer Consumer Products * Media, Entertainment & Sports * Retail, Apparel and Luxury Goods * Chief Marketing Officer >> Industrial Automotive and Transportation Equipment * Building Components * Chemical and Process Industries * Energy and CleanTech * Machinery and Engineering * Mining & Metals >> Services Supply Chain & Logistics * Travel & Hospitality * Business Services * Real Estate Services * Professional Services >> Private Equity Sovereign Wealth Funds >> Public and Social Sector Government and Regulatory * Intergovernmental and Multilateral Organizations * NGO, Charities and Foundations * Interest Representations and Associations * Academia and Education * Arts and Culture*

Minimum salary for assignments: $125,000
Retainer/AESC or MAJOR
Industries: most industries, industrial, aerospace, defense,
Positions: most positions, senior management, financial, human resources, information technology, MIS, attorneys, paralegals, marketing, logistics management, material management, purchasing, , international
www.egonzehnder.com

2099 Pennsylvania Avenue NW
Washington, DC 20006
202-774-1300/fax 202-774-1398
Mr. Olli Lauren , Partner /Olli.Lauren@egonzehnder.com
Mr. Neil Hindle , Partner /Neil.Hindle@ezi.net/ /industries GOV/NP/FIN/INS/positions GEN/SEN/RIS/HRS/LAW
Ms. Kim Henderson , Consultant /Kim.Henderson@ezi.net/ /industries CON/HSP/BRO/PUB/WWW/ENT/positions GEN/SEN/MIS/BOD
Mr. Manuel De Miranda , Managing Partner /Manuel.deMiranda@ezi.net/ /industries GEN/IND/AER/DEF/positions GEN/MIS/MAR/FIN/HRS/VEN
Ms. Kelly Emery , Associate /Kelly.Emery@egonzehnder.com/ /industries VEN/CNS/GOV/NP/positions GEN/MIS/MAR/FIN/HRS/VEN
Mr. Will Houston , Consultant /William.Houston@egonzehnder.com/ /industries IND/HIT/DEF/GOV/CMM/positions GEN/SEN/MIS/MAR/FIN/HRS
Ms. Jessica Watson , Consultant /Jessica.Watson@egonzehnder.com/ /industries HEA/BIO/NP/positions GEN/SEN/MIS/MAR/FIN/HRS

ELIASSEN GROUP, INC.

*From the website: Eliassen Group, Inc. -- We have been driving the success of our clients, consultants and employees with Technology Staffing and Consulting Services since 1989. For 25 years, we have been staffing and consulting leaders, perfectly matching capable and talented people with successful companies, helping them to attain their business objectives. Our solution oriented approach to understanding your needs ensures we identify and represent the best possible talent available in the market, personally selected and matched to your requirements by our highly-tenured, extraordinarily capable recruiting team. Our seasoned recruiters specialize in finding technical consultants with skill sets like these so we can offer our clients the expertise they need in hard-to-find categories, such as: * Application Development * Business Intelligence/Reporting * Database * Datawarehousing * ERP/SCM/CRM * Mainframe * Network/Infrastructure * Project Management * Quality Assurance * Statistical Programming * Business Systems Analysis * Technical Training/Support * Web Development/Design Sectors: * Technology Staffing * Agile Consulting * Biometrics * Government Services * Healthcare IT * Life*

Sciences Consulting * Workforce Management

Minimum salary for assignments: $50,000
Contingency search
Industries: most industries, hi-tech, biotechnology, bio-equipment, government, public administration, healthcare, hospitals
Positions: consulting, information technology, MIS, networks, LAN, WAN, , interim, contract, temporary placement
www.eliassen.com

6903 Rockledge Drive, Suite 810
Bethesda, MD 20817
301-365-8480
Mr. David Raff , Branch Director /DRaff@eliassen.com
Mr. Patrick Superko , Technical Recruiter /PSuperko@eliassen.com/ /industries GEN/HIT/BIO/GOV/HEA/positions CNS/MIS/NET/RND/TEM
Ms. Alice Boyle , Senior Account Executive /ABoyle@eliassen.com/ /industries GEN/HIT/BIO/GOV/HEA/positions CNS/MIS/NET/RND/TEM
Mr. Richard Moskowitz , Business Development Executive /RMoskowitz@eliassen.com/ /industries GEN/HIT/BIO/GOV/HEA/positions CNS/MIS/NET/RND/TEM
Ms. Sarah Pakrul , Technical Recruiter /SPakrul@eliassen.com/ /industries GEN/HIT/BIO/GOV/HEA/positions MIS/NET/TEM
Mr. Ronnie Miranda , Senior Account Executive /RMiranda@eliassen.com/ /industries GEN/HIT/BIO/GOV/HEA/positions MIS/NET/TEM
Mr. Zachary Hannon , Technical Recruiter /ZHannon@eliassen.com/ /industries GEN/HIT/BIO/GOV/HEA/positions MIS/NET/TEM

5523 Research Park Drive, Suite 115
Catonsville, MD 21228
443-636-2800
Mr. Kris Kurcoba , Vice President - Mid Atlantic /KKurcoba@eliassen.com
Mr. Mike Hume , Branch Director - Baltimore /MHume@eliassen.com/ /industries GEN/HIT/BIO/GOV/HEA/positions CNS/MIS/NET/RND/TEM
Ms. Brandi Saveri , Senior Technical Recruiter /BSaveri@eliassen.com/ /industries GEN/HIT/BIO/GOV/HEA/positions MIS/NET/TEM
Mr. Frank Yankellow , Senior Account Executive /FYankellow@eliassen.com/ /industries GEN/HIT/BIO/GOV/HEA/positions CNS/MIS/NET/RND/TEM
Mr. Andrew Raup , Senior Technical Recruiter /ARaup@eliassen.com/ /industries GEN/HIT/BIO/GOV/HEA/positions MIS/NET/TEM
Mr. Adam Jones , Senior Account Executive /AJones@eliassen.com/ /industries GEN/HIT/BIO/GOV/HEA/positions CNS/MIS/NET/RND/TEM
Mr. Alex Schuster , Technical Recruiter /ASchuster@eliassen.com/ /industries GEN/HIT/BIO/GOV/HEA/positions MIS/NET/TEM

EXECUQUEST CORP.

From the website: ExecuQuest Research Corp., www.eqcadvisors.com, has one driving mission: facilitating recruiting and search consultants to be the best you can be. With over three decades of successful client relationships, we are preferred providers of high-end talent sourcing, competitive organization chart development, research/market analysis and passive candidate development via targeted NLP telephone outreach, expert online sourcing and Search/Research Success(tm) by ExecuQuest training globally.

Minimum salary for assignments: $75,000
Retainer/AESC or MAJOR
Industries: financial services, manufacturing, services, healthcare, hospitals, consulting, management consulting
Positions: most positions, consulting, market research, product research
www.eqctalentsourcingexperts.com/home-2/

2413 Stanwick Road
Baltimore, MD 21131
410-667-8400
Ms. Conni LaDouceur , President /Conni@EQCTalentSourcingExperts.com
Ms. Donna Friedrich , Practice Leader /Donnna.F@EQCTalentSourcingExperts.com/ /industries FIN/MAN/SER/HEA/CSG/positions GEN/CNS/MRE
Ms. Melyssa Taganas , Senior Research Associate /Melyssa@eqcadvisors.com/ /industries FIN/MAN/SER/HEA/CSG/positions GEN/CNS/MRE

EXPERIS

From the website: More than ever, gaining competitive advantage and generating success depend on having the best experience and expertise in place in your organization. That's what Experis delivers. Going further than a typical professional services company, we connect you to both highly-skilled professionals and best-practice project solutions to address your challenges, accelerate your initiatives and help you seize opportunity. It's a powerful combination creating endless possibilities.

Minimum salary for assignments: $50,000
Contingency search
Industries: most industries, banking, financial services, biotechnology, bio-equipment, pharmaceuticals, drugs, biologicals, computers, software, consulting, management consulting, consumer, food and beverages insurance, e-commerce, internet, new media, utilities, retail trade
Positions: information technology, MIS, engineering, financial, accounting, medical, physicians, nurses, therapists, interim, contract, temporary placement
www.experis.com

One South Street, Suite 840
Baltimore, MD 21202
443-703-3800/fax 410-859-3867
Mr. Hil Andrews , Managing Director /Hil.Andrews@experis.com
Mr. Jude Rene , Technical Recruiter /Jude.Rene@experis.com/ /industries GEN/FIN/HEA/CON/WWW/RTL/positions MIS/NET/TEL/TEM
Mr. Eric Anderson , Business Development Manager /Eric.Anderson@experis.com/ /industries GEN/FIN/HEA/CON/WWW/RTL/positions MIS/NET/TEL/TEM
Mr. Brian Thornton , Talent Associate /Brian.Thornton@experis.com/ /industries GEN/FIN/HEA/CON/WWW/RTL/positions MIS/NET/TEL/TEM
Mr. Peter Dolan , Senior Technical Recruiter /Peter.Dolan@experis.com/ /industries GEN/FIN/HEA/CON/WWW/RTL/positions MIS/ENG/TEC/TEM

Mr. Jude Rene , Technical Recruiter /Jude.Rene@experis.com/ /industries GEN/FIN/HEA/CON/WWW/RTL/positions MIS/ENG/FIN/ACC/MED/TEM

FIDELIS CONSULTING GROUP

From the website: At Fidelis Consulting Group, we focus our efforts towards the recruitment of only the best associates and partner-level talent available. Our business revolves around law firms and corporate counsels interested in attracting attorneys with substantive abilities and high-profile reputations. We also assist attorneys with established practices and demonstrated business development skills explore alternative career paths.

Minimum salary for assignments: $100,000
Contingency search
Industries: most industries, law firms
Positions: attorneys, paralegals
www.fidelisgrp.com

Box 16978
Washington, DC 20041
571-223-1747
Mr. Brad Toynbee , Chief Executive Officer /BT@fidelisgrp.com

---

FURST GROUP

From the website: Furst Group possesses strong marketplace knowledge and longevity in the health care marketplace to help define executive talent for the new millennium. Furst Group shapes the future of health care by providing retained executive search to organizations and providers through a collaborative culture that maximizes the individual's talents, creativity and experience to exceed our stakeholders' expectations.

Minimum salary for assignments: $100,000
Retained search
Industries: biotechnology, bio-equipment, healthcare, hospitals, managed care, medical devices, pharmaceuticals, drugs, biologicals
Positions: accounting, administration, financial, human resources, marketing, medical, physicians, nurses, therapists, information technology, MIS, physicians, sales, senior management
www.furstgroup.com

2200 Pennsylvania Avenue NW
Washington, DC 20037
800-642-9940
Ms. Deanna Banks , Principal /DBanks@furstgroup.com

GM RYAN INTERNATIONAL

*From the website: GM Ryan is laser focused in a single professional sector - Digital Media & Internet Technologies. We consistently place C-level executives through Director level professionals as we specialize within the following industrial areas: Functions: * Executive * Sales & BD * Marketing * Product * Operations * Finance * Advertising * Analytics & Measurement * Client Services -- Verticals: * Digital Media * Ad-Tech * Data Sciences * Emerging Technologies * Internet Marketing * SaaS & Cloud Computing * eCommerce * Mobile * Venture Capital.*

Minimum salary for assignments: $50,000
Contingency search
Industries: e-commerce, internet, new media, advertising, public relations, information technology, computer services, data processing, wireless communications, venture capital/private equity
Positions: senior management, sales, marketing, operations, financial, advertising,
www.gmryan.com

47910 Woodmont Avenue
Bethesda, MD 20814
301-263-9505
Mr. Brian Mitchell , CEO & Managing Partner /Mitch@gmryan.com
Ms. Camilla McInnes , Director /Camilla@gmryan.com/ /industries BRO/WWW/WIR/positions SEN/SAL/MAR/OPS/FIN/RND
Ms. Gena Sikorsky , Partner /Gena@gmryan.com/ /industries WWW/ADV/DP/WIR/VEN/positions SEN/SAL/MAR/OPS/FIN/RND
Ms. Lisa Entzminger , Vice President of Operations /Lisa@gmryan.com/ /industries WWW/ADV/DP/WIR/VEN/positions SEN/SAL/MAR/OPS/FIN/RND

GARRISON & SISSON, INC.

From the website: Garrison & Sisson -- Since 1986, our recruiters have placed in excess of 1300 attorneys at law firms, including all of DC's 50 largest law firm offices and nearly every elite boutique. We also provide recruiting services to public, private and non-profit corporations in DC, Northern VA, and MD, and have placed over 350 attorneys in legal departments throughout this region. When you work with G&S, you benefit from aligning with DC's most powerful, respected, connected, and trusted attorney recruiters. Drawing on over 75 years of collective attorney recruiting experience, G&S recruiters offer encyclopedic knowledge of the DC metropolitan legal community. In short, we create an advantage for the attorney candidates & clients that work with us.

Minimum salary for assignments: $100,000
Contingency search
Industries: most industries, law firms
Positions: attorneys, paralegals
www.g-s.com

1627 I Street NW
Washington, DC 20006
202-429-5630

Mr. Martha Ann Sisson, Esq. , Partner /MASisson@g-s.com
Ms. Erin Sears, Esq. , Managing Director /ESears@g-s.com/ /industries GEN/LAW/positions LAW
Ms. Nancy Palermo, Esq. , Managing Partner /NPalermo@g-s.com/ /industries GEN/LAW/positions LAW
Ms. Justine Donahue, Esq. , Attorney Recruiter /JDonahue@g-s.com/ /industries GEN/LAW/positions LAW
Mr. Dan Binstock, Esq. , Partner /DBinstock@g-s.com/ /industries GEN/LAW/positions LAW
Mr. Matt Schwartz, Esq. , Partner /MSchwartz@g-s.com/ /industries GEN/LAW/positions LAW
Ms. Kaitlyn Isaac , Director of Operations /KIsaac@g-s.com/ /industries GEN/LAW/positions LAW

GREEN KEY RESOURCES

From the website: The Green Key executive recruitment team is uniquely suited to job placement in your industry because we've actually worked in it. We know what the demands are, where the jobs are, and we have exclusive relationships with some of the most sought-after employers around. Specialties: * Accounting/Finance * Alternative Asset Management * Financial Services * Healthcare * Human Resources * Information Technology * Legal * Office Support * Pharmaceutical * Temporary/Contract Recruitment.

Minimum salary for assignments: $40,000
Contingency search
Industries: accounting, financial services, venture capital/private equity, healthcare, hospitals, biotechnology, bio-equipment, pharmaceuticals, drugs, biologicals
Positions: accounting, financial, medical, physicians, nurses, therapists, human resources, information technology, MIS, attorneys, paralegals, administration, pharmacists, interim, contract, temporary placement
www.greenkeyllc.com

2275 Research Boulevard, Suite 350
Rockville, MD 20850
301-584-3186/fax 301-584-3196
Ms. Judy Holt , Executive Director /JHolt@greenkeyllc.com
Ms. Nicole Rusnak , Staffing Manager /NRusnak@greenkeyllc.com/ /industries GEN/ACC/FIN/VEN/HEA/GOV/positions ACC/FIN/HRS/MED/MIS/RND
Ms. Chelsea Gottleib , Recruiter /CGottleib@greenkeyllc.com/ /industries GEN/ACC/FIN/VEN/HEA/GOV/positions ACC/FIN/HRS/MED/MIS/RND
Ms. Kelly Lunacek , Director /KLunacek@greenkeyllc.com/ /industries ACC/FIN/VEN/HEA/BIO/PHR/positions MIS/NET
Ms. Karri Van damm , Senior Recruiter /KVandamm@greenkeyllc.com/ /industries ACC/FIN/VEN/HEA/BIO/PHR/positions ACC/FIN/HRS/MED/MIS/RND
Ms. Erika Silvey , Recruiter /ESilvey@greenkeyllc.com/ /industries ACC/FIN/VEN/HEA/BIO/PHR/positions ACC/FIN/HRS/MED/MIS/RND
Ms. Lauren Koubek , Director /LKoubek@greenkeyllc.com/ /industries GEN/ACC/FIN/VEN/HEA/GOV/positions ACC/FIN/AUD/TAX/CAS/CRE

HR STRATEGY GROUP

From the website: The mission of HR Strategy Group, LLC is to help small and mid-sized businesses and organizations with human resources advisory services. HR Strategy Group, LLC knows that business owners and executives need fast, effective and balanced solutions to their tough problems. We listen to our clients and understand the needs of their companies and provide customized, confidential and cost-effective services. Our superior Recruitment and Search process finds you the right candidate at a cost that is transparent, affordable and reasonable.

Minimum salary for assignments: $75,000
Retained search
Industries: most industries, government, public administration
Positions: most positions, senior management
www.hrstrategygroup.com

2810 Quail Creek Court
Ellicott City, MD 21042
410-505-8723
Ms. Amy Polefrone , President & Chief Executive Officer /Amy@hrstrategygroup.com
Ms. Donna Miracle , Chief Operating Officer /Donna@hrstrategygroup.com/ /industries GEN/GOV/positions GEN/SEN
Ms. Lindsay Moore, , Executive Vice President /Lindsay@hrstrategygroup.com/ /industries GEN/GOV/positions GEN/SEN
Ms. Katherine Sanford , Research Analyst /Katherine@hrstrategygroup.com/ /industries GEN/GOV/positions GEN/SEN
Ms. Karen Ward-Linker , Senior HR Consultant /Karen@hrstrategygroup.com/ /industries GEN/GOV/positions GEN/SEN
Ms. Nina Brown , Human Resources Consultant /Nina@hrstrategygroup.com/ /industries GEN/GOV/positions GEN/SEN

HAMILTON RYKER IT SOLUTIONS

From the website: Hamilton-Ryker manages Information Technology Infrastructure and provides staff augmentation, technical solutions and support for both the hardware and software components for our customer's enterprise computing environment including telephony, networks, servers, desktops and mobile computing.

Minimum salary for assignments: $50,000
Contingency search
Industries: most industries, automotive, motor vehicles, trucks, accounting, communications, telecommunications, banking, education, higher education, financial services, human resources services, manufacturing insurance
Positions: information technology, MIS, interim, contract, temporary placement
www.hamiltonrykerit.com

1725 Eye Street NW, 5th Floor
Washington, DC 20006
202-510-9345/fax 202-478-5238
Mr. L.J. Perry , Chief Information Officer /LJPerry@hamilton-ryker.com

---

HEIDRICK & STRUGGLES

From the website: As a premier professional services firm, Heidrick & Struggles continues to pioneer the fields of executive search, culture shaping and leadership consulting. We provide top organizations around the world with integrated solutions for all of their leadership needs. For more than 60 years we have helped our clients build the best leadership teams in the world. Our expertise comes from our ability to leverage our rich heritage while remaining vigilant to follow market trends that will affect the business landscape tomorrow. As the industry's pioneer, Heidrick & Struggles has been called on when the stakes are high. We help our clients change the world, one leadership team at a time(r).

Minimum salary for assignments: $175,000
Retainer/AESC or MAJOR
Industries: most industries, consumer, sports, hospitality, hotels, restaurants, entertainment, film, gaming, retail trade, education, higher education, non-profits, financial services, hi-tech, software, e-commerce, internet, new media industrial, biotechnology, bio-equipment
Positions: most positions, senior management, board of directors, human resources, financial, information technology, MIS, attorneys, paralegals, marketing, sales, logistics management, material management, purchasing international
www.heidrick.com

2001 Pennsylvania Avenue NW
Washington, DC 20006-1821
202-331-4900
Mr. Eric Joseph , Partner in Charge /EJoseph@heidrick.com
Mr. William O'Leary , Partner /BOLeary@heidrick.com/ /industries ED/NP/SEC/SER/positions GEN/BOD/SEN/MIS
Mr. Ron Brown , Partner /RBrown@heidrick.com/ /industries GEN/CON/NP/FIN/HIT/SFT/positions SEN/BOD/FIN
Mr. Randy Jayne , Partner /RJayne@heidrick.com/ /industries AER/DEF/ELC/SFT/WWW/NP/positions GEN/VEN/SEN/BOD
Mr. Daniel Edwards , Managing Partner /DEdwards@heidrick.com/ /industries VEN/INV/FIN/positions GEN/SEN/BOD
Mr. Julian Ha , Partner /JHa@heidrick.com/ /industries GOV/NP/positions SEN/BOD/DEV/MAR/SAL/LAW
Mr. Krishnan Rajagopalan , President and CEO /KRajagopalan@heidrick.com/ /industries ENR/ENV/VEN/WWW/positions GEN/SEN/MIS/VEN

HIGHSTREET IT SOLUTIONS, LLC

From the website: Highstreet provides enterprise application, cloud enablement, and management services - on premises, in the cloud or hybrid. At Highstreet, we know that you hired us to solve business problems. Our unmatched application expertise, technical know-how and results-driven approach have enabled more than 800 organizations to modernize their applications and infrastructure without disrupting their businesses.

Minimum salary for assignments: $50,000
Contingency search
Industries: most industries, government, public administration, e-commerce, internet, new media

Positions: information technology, MIS, networks, LAN, WAN, interim, contract, temporary placement
www.highstreetit.com

2600 Tower Oaks Boulevard, Suite 240
Rockville, MD 20852
703-263-1530
Mr. Greg Furst , Chief Executive Officer /Greg.Furst@highstreetit.com
Mr. Nick Magliato , Chief Operating Officer /Nick.Magliato@highstreetit.com/ /industries ED/GOV/WWW/positions MIS/NET/TEM
Mr. Alan Cook , Senior Vice President /Alan.Cook@highstreetit.com/ /industries GEN/GOV/WWW/positions MIS/NET/TEM
Ms. Christine Comai , Senior Recruiter /Christine.Comai@highstreetit.com/ /industries GEN/GOV/WWW/positions MIS/NET/TEM
Mr. Bill Cage , Executive Vice President and Practice Lead /Bill.Cage@highstreetit.com/ /industries HEA/FIN/NP/positions MIS/NET/TEM
Mr. Henry Tran , Executive Vice President and Practice Lead /Henry.Tran@highstreetit.com/ /industries ED/GOV/positions MIS/NET/TEM
Mr. Cecil Cadwallader , Executive Vice President, Sales /Cecil.Cadwallader@highstreetit.com/ /industries GEN/GOV/WWW/positions MIS/NET/TEM

HIRE COUNSEL

From the website: Hire Counsel is a leading innovative services provider to law firms, corporations and government agencies for today's new legal economy. Since 1993, Hire Counsel has helped our diversified clients manage dynamic workloads and distinct legal needs to achieve consistently superior results more profitably. Our commitment is to the highest quality standards, which we accomplish through the dedication of our people. Headquartered in New York City, Hire Counsel operates across all major legal centers in the U.S.

Minimum salary for assignments: $75,000
Contingency search
Industries: most industries, law firms
Positions: attorneys, paralegals, interim, contract, temporary placement
www.hirecounsel.com

1990 K Street NW
Washington, DC 20006
646-356-0550
Mr. Thomas Soha , Managing Director /TSoha@hirecounsel.com
Mr. Thomas Tessmer , Associate Director of Recruiting /TTessmer@hirecounsel.com/ /industries GEN/LAW/positions LAW/TEM
Ms. Lani Mark , Director of Business Services /LMark@hirecounsel.com/ /industries GEN/LAW/positions LAW/TEM

HIRESTRATEGY

From the website: HireStrategy is a full-service professional staffing firm providing consulting services, permanent placement, and executive search solutions for companies and career management in the technology, sales, finance and accounting professions. Our customers include Fortune 500, middle market and emerging growth companies across diverse industries.

Minimum salary for assignments: $50,000
Contingency search
Industries: most industries, government, public administration, financial services, environmental, green industries, education, higher education, hi-tech, non-profits
Positions: information technology, MIS, networks, LAN, WAN, telecommunications, sales, financial, accounting, interim, contract, temporary placement
www.hirestrategy.com

9711 Washingtonian Boulevard, Suite 450
Gaithersburg, MD 20878
240-630-1600
Ms. Daphne Wotherspoon , Managing Director /DWotherspoon@hirestrategy.com
Ms. Shelley Coombs , Branch Manager, Technology Contract Staffing /Shelley.Coombs@hirestrategy.com/ /industries GEN/GOV/FIN/ENV/NP/HIT/positions MIS/NET/TEL/TEM
Mr. Soulman Bushera , Senior Director /SBushera@hirestrategy.com/ /industries GEN/GOV/FIN/ENV/NP/HIT/positions MIS/NET/TEL/TEM
Mr. Alexander Santiago , Business Development Manager/ /ASantiago@hirestrategy.com/ /industries GEN/GOV/FIN/ENV/NP/HIT/positions ACC/FIN/AUD/TAX/CAS/CRE
Ms. Adrienne Frandsen , Recruiting Manager /AFrandsen@hirestrategy.com/ /industries GEN/GOV/FIN/ENV/NP/HIT/positions MIS/NET/TEL/SAL/FIN/ACC
Ms. Emily Walsh , Sales Manager, Finance & Accounting /EWalsh@hirestrategy.com/ /industries GEN/GOV/FIN/ENV/NP/HIT/positions ACC/FIN/AUD/TAX/CAS/CRE
Ms. Ashley Cima , Senior Director, Business Development /ACima@hirestrategy.com/ /industries GEN/GOV/FIN/ENV/NP/HIT/positions MIS/NET/TEL/SAL/FIN/ACC

1121 14th Street NW, Suite 600
Washington, DC 20005
202-527-7800
Mr. Josh Fisher , Senior Vice President /JFisher@HireStrategy.com
Mr. Shawn Redwine , Senior Consultant /Shawn.Redwine@hirestrategy.com/ /industries GEN/GOV/FIN/ENV/ED/HIT/positions MIS/NET/TEL
Ms. Alana Hyman , Senior Director /AHyman@hirestrategy.com/ /industries GEN/GOV/FIN/ENV/ED/HIT/positions MIS/NET/TEL/TEM
Ms. Cassandra Monk , Vice President, Business Development /CMonk@hirestrategy.com/ /industries GEN/GOV/FIN/ENV/ED/HIT/positions MIS/NET/TEL/TEM
Mr. Eric Klein , Senior Vice President, Technology /EKlein@hirestrategy.com/ /industries GEN/GOV/FIN/ENV/ED/HIT/positions MIS/NET/TEL/TEM
Ms. Barbara Wallace , Managing Director /BWallace@hirestrategy.com/ /industries GEN/GOV/FIN/ENV/ED/HIT/positions MIS/NET/TEL/SAL/FIN/ACC
Ms. Daphne Wotherspoon , Managing Director /DWotherspoon@hirestrategy.com/ /industries GEN/GOV/FIN/ENV/ED/HIT/positions MIS/NET/TEL/SAL/FIN/ACC

HURON CONSULTING GROUP

From the website: Huron is a global professional services firm committed to achieving sustainable results in partnership with our clients. We bring a depth of expertise in strategy, operations, advisory services, technology and analytics to drive lasting and measurable results in the healthcare, higher education, life sciences and commercial sectors. Through focus, passion and collaboration, Huron provides guidance to support organizations as they contend with the change transforming their industries and businesses.

Minimum salary for assignments: $100,000
Retained search
Industries: healthcare, hospitals
Positions: consulting
www.huronconsultinggroup.com

1620 L Street NW
Washington, DC 20036
202-585-1699
Ms. Neera Gupta , Managing Director /NGupta@huronconsultinggroup.com
Mr. Ted Simpson , Managing Director /TSimpson@huronconsultinggroup.com/ /industries ED/positions CNS
Ms. Leah Guidry , Managing Director /LGuidry@huronconsultinggroup.com/ /industries HEA/positions CNS
Ms. Kimberly Trubenbacher , Director, Recruiting Operations /KTrubenbacher@huronconsultinggroup.co/ /industries CSG/positions MIS

ISAACSON, MILLER

From the website: Isaacson, Miller has recruited leadership for the full array of public purposes since 1982. Currently, more than 60% of the firm's work is in higher education, and many of our other fields are listed below. Most of our searches are for CEOs, presidents, and other senior executives. We also have one of the largest advancement and fundraising practices in the nation. Representative Fields: * Advancement & Fundraising * Healthcare * Advocacy * Higher Education * Arts & Culture * Human Services * Associations * International Aid & Development * Conservation & Environment * PreK-12 Education * Economic & Community Development * Scientific Research & Policy Institutes * Foundations.

Minimum salary for assignments: $120,000
Retainer/AESC or MAJOR
Industries: education, higher education, healthcare, hospitals, non-profits
Positions: most positions, board of directors, development, fund raising, marketing, , senior management
www.imsearch.com

1300 19th Street NW
Washington, DC 20036
202-682-1504
Ms. Jane Gruenebaum , Vice President and Director /JGruenebaum@imsearch.com
Ms. Ericka Miller , Partner /EMiller@imsearch.com/ /industries ED/HEA/NP/positions GEN/BOD/DEV/MAR/RND/SEN
Ms. Ponneh Varho , Partner /PVarho@imsearch.com/ /industries ED/HEA/NP/positions GEN/BOD/DEV/MAR/RND/SEN

Mr. Michael Baer , Partner /MBaer@imsearch.com/ /industries ED/positions GEN/BOD/DEV/MAR/RND/SEN
Mr. Tim McFeeley , Partner /TMcFeeley@imsearch.com/ /industries ED/HEA/NP/positions GEN/BOD/DEV/MAR/RND/SEN
Ms. Jacqueline Mildner , Partner /JMildner@imsearch.com/ /industries ED/HEA/NP/positions GEN/BOD/DEV/MAR/RND/SEN
Ms. Pam Pezzoli , Partner /PPezzoli@imsearch.com/ /industries ED/HEA/NP/positions GEN/BOD/DEV/MAR/RND/SEN

JDG ASSOCIATES LTD.

From the website: JDG Associates consistently ranks among the most highly-respected executive search firms in the Washington, D.C. region. During our almost 40-year history as a privately-owned firm, we have developed expertise in virtually every major industry and functional discipline. Our local and national clients include prominent research and consulting organizations; Fortune 1000 corporations; federal, state and local government agencies; as well as associations and non-profit organizations. Active Searches: Contracting Officers * Cost Analysts * Director, HIV/AIDS Twinning Center Program * Director, Public Sector IT Consulting * National Sales Director, Membership and Services * President and CEO * Principal (Federal Finance, Regulatory and Compliance) * Principal Education Research Scientist * Public Sector Data Analytics Director * Research Director, Health Policy * Senior Manager - Federal Financial Management * Senior Research Associate - Education * Senior Research Associate - Human Services * Senior Research Associate - Labor * Senior/Principal Associate (Community Science) * Vice President of Survey Research * Vice President, Electric & Gas Utility Consulting

Minimum salary for assignments: $65,000
Contingency search
Industries: most industries, government, public administration, non-profits
Positions: marketing, sales, public relations, engineering, financial, information technology, MIS, human resources, senior management
www.jdgsearch.com

1700 Research Boulevard
Rockville, MD 20850
301-340-2210
Mr. Darren DeGioia , President /Darren.DeGioia@jdgsearch.com
Mr. Joe DeGioia , Executive Advisor /DeGioia@jdgsearch.com/ /industries GEN/GOV/NP/positions SEN/MAR/SAL/FIN/HRS/MIS
Mr. Paul Belford , Principal and Director /Belford@jdgsearch.com/ /industries NP/positions SEN/MAR/SAL/FIN/HRS/MIS
Mr. Anthony Brown , Principal /Brown@jdgsearch.com/ /industries GEN/GOV/NP/positions SEN/MAR/SAL/FIN/HRS/MIS
Ms. Angela Goehl , Associate /Goehl@jdgsearch.com/ /industries NP/positions SEN/MAR/SAL/FIN/HRS/MIS
Ms. Alison Marshall , Principal /Marshall@jdgsearch.com/ /industries GOV/positions RND/MIS

KINCANNON & REED

From the website: Kincannon & Reed is a retained executive search firm engaged by organizations around the world to recruit impact players in the food, agribusiness, and life sciences sectors. Clients benefit from our unique focus, expertise, and approach. This combination has produced an enviable record of success: we deliver leaders with judgment who get results.

Minimum salary for assignments: $150,000
Retainer/AESC or MAJOR
Industries: agriculture, agribusiness, biotechnology, bio-equipment, chemicals, environmental, green industries, food and beverages, pharmaceuticals, drugs, biologicals
Positions: most positions, engineering, financial, international, manufacturing, marketing, , technical, scientific, senior management
www.krsearch.com

Washington, DC
703-623-3961
Mr. Jay Andre , Senior Director /JAndre@krsearch.net
Mr. Greg Dooman , Senior Associate /GDooman@krsearch.net/ /industries AGR/BIO/CHM/ENV/FOD/PHR/positions GEN/ENG/FIN/MAN/MAR/SEN

KINGSLEY GATE PARTNERS

From the website: From Fortune 500s to rocketing start-ups, companies of all sizes and from all sectors come to Kingsley Gate Partners for access to the right high-level, high-powered leaders for their most critical hires. Private equity firms, venture capitalists, portfolio companies as well as high-profile executives and CEOs regard Kingsley Gate as a precise advantage. They understand that the best constructed team directly leads to creating the widest radius of success - and that Kingsley Gate is the most direct way to capture those advantages

Minimum salary for assignments: $100,000
Retained search
Industries: investment banks, merchant banks, venture capital/private equity, hi-tech, broadcasting, media, TV, radio, cable TV, e-commerce, internet, new media, wireless communications, information technology, computer services, data processing communications, telecommunications, software, consumer, biotechnology, bio-equipment, medical devices, retail trade
Positions: most positions, board of directors, venture capital
www.kingsleygate.com

Baltimore, MD
202-930-4322
Mr. Buster Houchins , Partner /BHouchins@kingsleygate.com
Ms. Lisa Pulay , Director /LPulay@kingsleygate.com/ /industries VEN/HIT/CMM/FIN/BIO/MDE/positions GEN/BOD/VEN

3 Bethesda Metro Center, Suite 700
Bethesda, MD 20814
202-741-9199
Ms. Nancy Albertini , Senior Partner /NAlbertini@kingsleygate.com

KORN FERRY

From the website: Korn Ferry -- We know the pressure you're under to find leaders who fit in with your organization and make it stand out. Korn Ferry offers the most validated search approach, deep knowledge of your industry, and innovative science and analytics. So you can make the best possible decision for the long term, the first time. Attracting top talent can be time-consuming, costly, and complex, but science and analytics can simplify and accelerate your search while mitigating risk. No one knows more about the science of performance than Korn Ferry. Our innovative search process includes proprietary tools like our Four Dimensional Executive Assessment and Executive Snapshot, giving you assurance that you are selecting the candidate with the right skills, qualifications, and values for the job, and compensating them appropriately.

Minimum salary for assignments: $125,000
Retainer/AESC or MAJOR
Industries: most industries, agriculture, agribusiness, broadcasting, media, TV, radio, cable TV, energy, environmental, green industries, equipment, machinery, financial services, healthcare, hospitals, hi-tech, non-profits retail trade, wireless communications, e-commerce, internet, new media
Positions: most positions, board of directors, engineering, financial, human resources, manufacturing, medical, physicians, nurses, therapists, marketing, market research, product research, information technology, MIS , senior management, technical, scientific
www.kornferry.com

1700 K Street NW
Washington, DC 20006
202-822-9444
Mr. Michael Hyter , Managing Director /Michael.Hyter@kornferry.com
Ms. Divina Gamble , Senior Client Partner /Divina.Gamble@kornferry.com/ /industries ED/NP/positions GEN/DEV/SEN
Mr. Charles Ingersoll, Jr. , Senior Client Partner /Charles.Ingersoll@kornferry.com/ /industries GOV/NP/ED/positions GEN/SEN
Mr. Clarke Havener , Global Sector Leader /Clarke.Havener@kornferry.com/ /industries AER/DEF/IND/positions GEN/SEN
Ms. Beth Fowler , Senior Client Partner /Beth.Fowler@kornferry.com/ /industries GOV/positions GEN/SEN
Ms. Maureen Ryan , Senior Client Partner /Maureen.Ryan@kornferry.com/ /industries HEA/positions GEN/PHY/SEN
Mr. Alex Martin , Global Sector Leader, Industrial Manufact. /Alex.Martin@kornferry.com/ /industries CHM/ENR/MAN/IND/positions GEN/MAN/ENG/SEN

KORN FERRY FUTURESTEP

From the website: Futurestep is the global industry leader in high-impact recruitment solutions, offering fully customized, flexible strategies to help organizations meet specific workforce needs. Our clients turn to us for proven expertise, a global process and infrastructure, proprietary competency models, innovative sourcing strategies, and a unique approach to measuring and optimising business impact. We offer RPO, project recruitment, individual search, talent consulting and employer branding services - all backed by the industry-leading insights and methodologies of our parent company, Korn/Ferry. Sectors: * Consumer and Retail * Financial Services * Government and Not for Profit * Industrial and Manufacturing * Life Sciences * Technology

Minimum salary for assignments: $75,000
Retained search
Industries: consumer, retail trade, financial services, government, public administration, non-profits, industrial, manufacturing, biotechnology, bio-equipment, hi-tech, construction, energy, automotive, motor vehicles, trucks defense, transportation
Positions: operations, marketing, human resources, sales, financial, risk management, information technology, MIS, logistics management, material management, purchasing, medical, physicians, nurses, therapists , international, interim, contract, temporary placement
www.futurestep.com

1700 K Street NW
Washington, DC 20006
202-822-9444
Ms. Rachel Flaim , Recruitment Partner /Rachel.Flaim@futurestep.com
Mr. Brian Black , Senior Recruiter /Brian.Black@kornferry.com/ /industries ELC/MAN/positions ENG/MIS/TEC
Mr. John Swirchak , Director /John.Swirchak@futurestep.com/ /industries GOV/DEF/CON/HIT/RTL/MAN/positions GEN/MAR/HRS/FIN/LOG/MAN
Mr. Jorge Herrera , Managing Consultant /Jorge.Herrera@futurestep.com/ /industries GOV/DEF/CON/HIT/RTL/MAN/positions GEN/MAR/HRS/FIN/LOG/MAN
Ms. Emily Mattson , Recruitment Partner RPO /Emily.Mattson@futurestep.com/ /industries PHR/BIO/MDE/positions GEN/MAR/HRS/FIN/LOG/MAN
Ms. Christina Quintero-Elstro , Senior Recruiting Consultant /Christina.Quintero-Elstro@futurestep.com/ /industries CMM/WIR/positions GEN/MAR/HRS/FIN/LOG/MIS
Ms. Sholeh Shirazi , Client Manager /Sholeh.Shirazi@futurestep.com/ /industries SEC/positions GEN/MAR/HRS/FIN/SEC/MIS

KOYA LEADERSHIP PARTNERS

From the website: Koya Leadership Partners is a national retained search firm that focuses on the non-profit sector. We are committed to our clients and to the missions that they serve. We deliver measurable results, finding exceptionally talented people who truly fit the unique culture of our client organizations. Not-for-Profit Sectors: * Education/Youth * Health Care * Environmental * Social Justice * Social Services * Women & Girls Advocacy.

Minimum salary for assignments: $75,000
Retained search
Industries: non-profits
Positions: most positions, senior management, development, fund raising
www.koyapartners.com

1875 Connecticut Avenue NW
Washington, DC 20009
866-282-0955
Ms. Turner Delano , Managing Director /TDelano@koyapartners.com

LATERAL LINK

From the website: Lateral Link is a full-service legal recruitment firm specializing in legal searches for AmLaw 200 and boutique law firms. We recruit in major legal markets in the United States and across Asia. We are a legal recruiting firm that attracts the best candidates seeking opportunities with the best clients; and top clients seeking access to top candidates.

Minimum salary for assignments: $100,000
Contingency search
Industries: most industries, law firms
Positions: attorneys, paralegals
www.laterallink.com

5613 River View Drive
Washington, DC 22310
703-937-7023
Ms. Amy Savage , Principal /ASavage@laterallink.com

LUCAS GROUP

From the website: Lucas Group's management recruiters offer candidates and client companies personal service, confidentiality and the most ethical, professional standards in the recruiting industry. Lucas Group is the premiere executive recruiting partner in assisting mid-tier to Fortune 500 companies around the nation find transcendent talent. Our Practice Groups specialize in Accounting, Finance, Human Resources, Legal, Manufacturing, Marketing, Military Transition, Sales, and Technology We recruit for positions from Managers to C-level executives. The majority of our placements are from Director and Vice President levels. Our Practice Groups specialize in Accounting, Finance, Human Resources, Legal, Manufacturing, Marketing, Military Transition, Sales, and Technology

Minimum salary for assignments: $75,000
Contingency search
Industries: most industries, law firms
Positions: attorneys, paralegals, interim, contract, temporary placement
www.lucasgroup.com

One Village Square
Baltimore, MD 21210
410-323-0400
Mr. C. Thomas Williamson, III , General Manager, Legal Division /TWilliamson@lucasgroup.com
Mr. Kevin Flynn , Senior Executive Search Consultant /KFlynn@lucasgroup.com/ /industries GEN/LAW/positions LAW/TEM
Ms. Robin Wexler , Executive Senior Partner /RWexler@lucasgroup.com/ /industries GEN/LAW/positions LAW/TEM
Ms. Sherri Thomas , Director /SThomas@lucasgroup.com/ /industries GEN/LAW/positions LAW/TEM
Mr. Steve Sarigianis , Executive Senior Partner /SSarigianis@lucasgroup.com/ /industries

GEN/LAW/positions LAW/TEM
Ms. Karissa Hayko , Assistant Manager - Contract /KHayko@lucasgroup.com/ /industries
GEN/LAW/positions LAW/TEM

1110 Vermont Avenue NW
Washington, DC 20005
202-292-6920
Mr. Carl White , Executive Senior Partner /CWhite@lucasgroup.com
Ms. Anna Wheeler , Senior Partner /AWheeler@lucasgroup.com/ /industries
GEN/CMM/CMP/FIN/HEA/SFT/positions HRS
Mr. Mike Christ , Executive Senior Partner /MChrist@lucasgroup.com/ /industries
GEN/CMM/CMP/FIN/HEA/SFT/positions MAR/SAL/MAN/LOG/PUR/OPS
Ms. Ann Reiling , Managing Partner /AReiling@lucasgroup.com/ /industries
GEN/CMM/CMP/FIN/HEA/SFT/positions HRS
Ms. Robin Wexler , Executive Senior Partner /RWexler@lucasgroup.com/ /industries
GEN/LAW/positions LAW
Ms. Laura Maxwell , Senior Partner /LMaxwell@lucasgroup.com/ /industries
GEN/CMM/CMP/FIN/HEA/SFT/positions MAR/SAL/MAN/LOG/PUR/OPS
Ms. Miranda Reed , Branch Manager /MReed@lucasgroup.com/ /industries
GEN/CMM/CMP/FIN/HEA/SFT/positions ACC/FIN/AUD/TAX/CRE/CAS

MJ MORGAN GROUP

From the website: With offices in downtown Baltimore, MD and Hyattsville, MD; MJ Morgan Group is one of the "Largest Professional Search Firms," and "Largest Temporary Staffing Agencies" as awarded by Baltimore Business Journal. We serve clients throughout the Mid-Atlantic region and beyond. MJ Morgan Group hires for positions in a wide range of levels - from assistants to the C-suite - with a common goal of finding the best people for the right job. Our specialties include Healthcare, IT, Engineering, Sales, Marketing, Accounting, Administrative, and Light Industrial. No matter your employment needs, MJ Morgan Group can provide you with innovative solutions - and top talents - that will save your company both time and money.

Minimum salary for assignments: $50,000
Contingency search
Industries: most industries, healthcare, hospitals, government, public administration
Positions: medical, physicians, nurses, therapists, information technology, MIS, engineering, sales, marketing, accounting, administration, industrial labor, interim, contract, temporary placement
www.mjmorgangroup.com

205 Harborview Drive
Baltimore, MD 21230
410-605-0090
Mr. Michael Morgan , President /Michael.Morgan@mjmorgangroup.com
Mr. Patrick Cosgrove , Vice President /Patrick.Cosgrove@mjmorgangroup.com/ /industries
GEN/HEA/GOV/positions MED/MIS/ENG/SAL/MAR/ACC
MS. Emily Wise , Recruiter /Emily.Wise@mjmorgangroup.com/ /industries
GEN/HEA/GOV/positions MED/MIS/ENG/SAL/MAR/ACC
Ms. Melonie Chinn , Recruiting Manager, Accounting & Finance
/Melonie.Chinn@mjmorgangroup.com/ /industries GEN/HEA/GOV/positions
ACC/FIN/AUD/TAX/CAS/CRE

Mr. James Fender , Division Director, Accounting & Finance
/James.Fender@mjmorgangroup.com/ /industries GEN/HEA/GOV/positions
ACC/FIN/AUD/TAX/CAS/CRE
Mr. Brian Sheridan , Business Development /Brian.Sheridan@mjmorgangroup.com/ /industries
GEN/HEA/GOV/positions MED/MIS/ENG/SAL/MAR/ACC
Ms. Shannon Tehan , Recruiter /Shannon.Tehan@mjmorgangroup.com/ /industries
GEN/HEA/GOV/positions MED/MIS/ENG/SAL/MAR/ACC

MADOLE LEGAL SEARCH

From the website: Madole Legal Search specializes in Washington, D.C. focused legal recruiting of top attorneys with law firms and companies. The Washington legal market is sophisticated and academically competitive. It ebbs and flows as a function of the overall economy and due to supply and demand influences that are unique to Washington. Whether you are a candidate, law firm or company, working with a D.C. based legal recruiter who has extensive experience in the DC legal market is critical to ensure an effective, time efficient and ultimately successful search.

Minimum salary for assignments: $100,000
Contingency search
Industries: most industries, law firms
Positions: attorneys, paralegals
www.madolelegalsearch.com

4410 Massachusetts Avenue
Washington, DC 20016
202-331-3821
Ms. Sadie Madole, Esq. , Owner /SMadole@madolelegalsearch.com

---

MAJOR, LINDSEY & AFRICA

From the website: Major, Lindsey & Africa is unmatched in the legal talent we attract, the services that we provide and the global reach we possess. With recruitment office locations from Sydney to San Francisco and from Houston to Hong Kong, we have a global network of deeply experienced legal recruiters and consultants who are skilled at pinpointing the professionals and the opportunities that optimize careers, teams and organizations. For more than 35 years, the world's leading law firms, lawyers and corporations have chosen Major, Lindsey & Africa to help them navigate the legal landscape.

Minimum salary for assignments: $100,000
Retainer/AESC or MAJOR
Industries: most industries, law firms
Positions: attorneys, paralegals, interim, contract, temporary placement
www.mlaglobal.com

7317 Parkway Drive South
Hanover, MD 21076

410-540-7087/fax 410-694-5272
Ms. Kristin Lyon , Senior Manager, Head Of Research /KLyon@mlaglobal.com
Mr. Stephen Forman , Chief Financial Officer /SForman@mlaglobal.com/ /industries GEN/LAW/positions LAW
Mr. William Mooney , Managing Director /WMooney@mlaglobal.com/ /industries GEN/LAW/positions LAW
Ms. Randi Lewis , Managing Director /RLewis@mlaglobal.com/ /industries GEN/LAW/positions LAW

600 Thirteenth Street NW
Washington, DC 20005
202-628-0660/fax 202-628-0696
Mr. Jeffrey Lowe , Managing Partner /JLowe@mlaglobal.com
Ms. Nancy Newkirk , Managing Director /NNewkirk@mlaglobal.com/ /industries GEN/LAW/positions LAW
Ms. Jane Roberts , Partner /JRoberts@mlaglobal.com/ /industries GEN/LAW/positions LAW
Ms. Lauren Drake , Managing Director /LDrake@mlaglobal.com/ /industries GEN/LAW/positions LAW
Ms. Deborah Ben-Canaan , Partner /DBenCanaan@mlaglobal.com/ /industries GEN/LAW/positions LAW
Mr. Mark Yacano , Global Practice Leader /MYacano@mlaglobal.com/ /industries GEN/LAW/positions LAW
Mr. Stephen Springer , Partner /SSpringer@mlaglobal.com/ /industries GEN/LAW/positions LAW

MATCHSTAR VENTURE SEARCH

From the website: For over a decade and a half, MatchStar has successfully placed hundreds of VP, Director and C-level executives into core leadership positions at the most innovative, venture backed companies in the world. We are a semi-retained, performance driven executive search firm that overcomes the limitations of the fully retained search model - expensive fees, large deposits, limited candidates, and long lead times.

Minimum salary for assignments: $75,000
Contingency search
Industries: hi-tech, biotechnology, bio-equipment, communications, telecommunications, e-commerce, internet, new media, software, environmental, green industries
Positions: most positions, information technology, MIS, financial, human resources, marketing, sales, venture capital, senior management
www.matchstar.com

1803 Research Boulevard
Rockville, MD 20850
301-802-2094
Ms. Heidi Hansen , SVP Operations & Research /Heidi@matchstar.com
Mr. Adrian Harrison , Research Specialist /Adrian@matchstar.com/ /industries HIT/BIO/CMM/WWW/SFT/ENV/positions GEN/MIS/FIN/HRS/MAR/SAL

MEDICAL STAFFING NETWORK

From the website: Medical Staffing Network wants to offer you more in a healthcare job, travel or per diem. As one of the largest and most recognized healthcare staffing brands in the industry, Medical Staffing Network has the depth and resources to offer you more healthcare job options to accommodate your career needs at any point in your life - whether it be travel or per diem nursing. From travel assignments of 13 to 26 weeks, per diem opportunities and local contracts - we can offer you true flexibility with dependability. Our travel and per diem job database is growing and changing every day, which can keep you working for as long or short as you would like.

Minimum salary for assignments: $35,000
Contingency search
Industries: healthcare, hospitals
Positions: most positions, administration, laboratory personnel, nursing, pharmacists, therapists, interim, contract, temporary placement
www.msnhealth.com

8115 Maple Lawn
Fulton, MD 20759
301-960-1088/fax 301-572-2126
Mr. Gregory Hart , Healthcare Recruiter /GregoryHart@msnhealth.com

1122 Kenilworth Drive
Towson, MD 21204
410-821-8001/fax 866-561-9945
Ms. Brittany Bowman , Recruiter /BrittanyBowman@msnhealth.com
Ms. Catie Makowske /CatieMakowske@msnhealth.com/ /industries HEA/positions GEN/ADM/LAB/NUR/PHR/THE

MEE DERBY & COMPANY

From the website: Mee Derby & Company is the nation's premier search firm specializing in Staffing, Professional Services and Workforce Solutions. We staff the staffing industry. Mee Derby is a leader among the handful of companies in the United States that staffs the staffing industry. We are one of the oldest and largest "recruitment-to-recruitment" firms. Our commitment to the industry is enhanced by active involvement and leadership in leading industry trade associations.

Minimum salary for assignments: $50,000
Contingency search
Industries: human resources services
Positions: most positions, human resources, sales, senior management, interim, contract, temporary placement
www.meederby.com

6620 81st Street
Cabin John, MD 20818
301-263-2663
Ms. Robin Mee , President /Robin@meederby.com

Ms. Kim Whiteley , Director and Executive Recruiter /Kim@meederby.com/ /industries HRS/positions GEN/HRS/SAL/SEN/TEM
Ms. Eliza Deang , Operations Manager /Eliza@MeeDerby.com/ /industries HRS/positions GEN/HRS/SAL/SEN/TEM
Ms. Jade Mannings , Executive Recruiter /Jade@meederby.com/ /industries HRS/positions GEN/HRS/SAL/SEN/TEM
Ms. Cole Moore , Executive Recruiter /Cole@meederby.com/ /industries HRS/positions GEN/HRS/SAL/SEN/TEM
Ms. Sue Jagan , Executive Recruiter /Sue@meederby.com/ /industries HRS/positions GEN/HRS/SAL/SEN/TEM
Ms. Suzanne Gates , Executive Recruiter /Suzanne@meederby.com/ /industries HRS/positions GEN/HRS/SAL/SEN/TEM

THE MERCER GROUP, INC.

From the website: The Mercer Group, Inc. is an independent management consulting firm incorporated in the State of Georgia and operating nationwide. The firm was founded by James L. Mercer, a management consultant of more than 30 years in the public and private sectors and a former Assistant City Manager. He has written or co-authored seven books and more than 300 articles on various phases of public management. The Mercer Group provides the highest quality management consulting services to federal, state and local governments and to health care providers, transit authorities, utilities, and private-sector clients.

Minimum salary for assignments: $75,000
Retained search
Industries: education, higher education, government, public administration, non-profits
Positions: most positions, administration, consulting, human resources, senior management
www.mercergroupinc.com

15 Cambridge Place
Ocean Pines, MD 21811
301-343-6033
Mr. David Deutsch , Senior Vice President /DavidDeutsch610@gmail.com

---

MESTEL & COMPANY

From the website: Since 1987, Mestel & Company has redefined professionalism, knowledge and service in the permanent attorney placement industry. Our experienced recruiters and first-hand knowledge of the practices and cultures of law firms and in-house legal departments have made us the acknowledged leader in our field. We place associates, partners and counsel and facilitate complex department and firm mergers.

Minimum salary for assignments: $100,000
Contingency search
Industries: most industries, law firms
Positions: attorneys, paralegals

www.mestel.com

1725 I Street NW
Washington, DC 20036
202-524-6360/fax 202-315-0516
Mr. Howard Parris, Esq. , Executive Managing Director /HParris@mestel.com
Ms. Cindy Finn, Esq. , Senior Director /CFinn@mestel.com/ /industries GEN/LAW/positions LAW
Mr. Christian Wickwire, Esq. , Senior Executive Director /SCWickwire@mestel.com/ /industries GEN/LAW/positions LAW
Ms. Karen Pate, Esq. , Senior Director /KPate@mestel.com/ /industries GEN/LAW/positions LAW

THE MEYERS GROUP

From the website:The Meyers Group is dedicated to meeting your permanent and temporary staffing needs in the Behavioral Health and Community Health/FQHC industries. The Meyers Group specializes in permanent and interim placement of professionals in the following industries: * Behavioral Healthcare * Community Healthcare & Primary Care * Managed Care * Accounting and Financial Services * Healthcare General * Rehabilitation and Long-Term Acute Care Systems * Succession Planning to Boards and CEOs.

Minimum salary for assignments: $45,000
Contingency search
Industries: biotechnology, bio-equipment, healthcare, hospitals, managed care, pharmaceuticals, drugs, biologicals
Positions: most positions, financial, marketing, medical, physicians, nurses, therapists, information technology, MIS, physicians, sales, senior management, interim, contract, temporary placement
www.mr-themeyersgroup.com

11700 Old Georgetown Road
North Bethesda, MD 20852
301-625-5600/fax 301-625-0138
Dr. Stuart Meyers , President /SIM@mr-themeyersgroup.com
Mr. Ron Morton , Vice President, Healthcare Division /RWM@mr-themeyersgroup.com/ /industries HEA/positions GEN
Ms. Michelle Carrigan , Internet Researcher /MMC@mr-themeyersgroup.com/ /industries BIO/HEA/MCA/PHR/positions GEN

MILLENNIUM CORPORATION

From the website: Millennium Corporation is an 8(a) certified Small Disadvantaged Business (SDB) and Service Disabled Veteran Owned Small Business (SDVOSB) established in 2004 as a professional services and management solutions partner offering world class integrated business solutions for all levels of government and commercial enterprises. Our core competencies include: * Program Management (DAWIA III/PMI) * Acquisition Management * Contract Management * Logistics Solutions * Financial Management * Human Resources Consulting * Information

Technology * Lean Six Sigma * Systems Engineering Support * Earned Value Management * Capabilities & Requirements Support.

Minimum salary for assignments: $50,000
Contingency search
Industries: government, public administration
Positions: project management, logistics management, material management, financial, information technology, MIS, engineering, interim, contract, temporary placement
www.millgroupinc.com

4692 Millennium Drive, Suite 305
Belcamp, MD 21017
703-436-1343/fax 703-914-9493
Mr. Kevin Jennings, President & Chief Executive Officer /Kevin.Jennings@millgroupinc.com

---

MILLERBLOWERS

From the website: MillerBlowers, Inc. has assisted the East Coast's most prestigious law firms and corporations with strategic growth for nearly four decades. Our legal recruiters provide deep institutional knowledge to clients and candidates, helping them to avoid the pitfalls inherent in the hiring process. MillerBlowers conducts business the right way. Our company strictly adheres to NALSC standards and its own rules relating to contacts and dealings with law firms, corporations and attorneys. Because of this, MillerBlowers is the legal recruiter of choice for dozens of AmLaw 100 firms and Global 1000 corporations, as well as smaller law firms, specialty boutiques and emerging companies.

Minimum salary for assignments: $100,000
Contingency search
Industries: most industries, law firms
Positions: attorneys, paralegals
www.millerlawjobs.com

9301 Gunpowder Place
Montgomery Village, MD 20886
202-640-2130
Ms. Tracy Mohr, Director, Washington DC Office /Tracy@millerblowers.com

---

MINDFINDERS, INC.

From the website: MindFinders, Inc., a leader in providing mission-critical solutions, has extensive experience in providing high-quality staffing and IT project solutions to the federal government, state governments, and Fortune 500 corporations. As one of the leading staffing firms in Washington DC, we are dedicated to providing total solutions and assisting our clients with a wide range of management support functions to meet unique and evolving needs. Whether you're a client looking for reliable staffing agencies, or a candidate looking for jobs hiring in DC or surrounding areas, MindFinders can help you reach your goals.

Minimum salary for assignments: $50,000
Contingency search
Industries: most industries, government, public administration, non-profits
Positions: information technology, MIS, networks, LAN, WAN, telecommunications, accounting, administration, interim, contract, temporary placement
www.themindfinders.com

1200 18th Street NW, Suite 550
Washington, DC 20036
202-400-2602/fax 202-450-5693
Mr. Tim Booker , Founder, President & CEO /TBooker@themindfinders.com
Mr. Corey Miller , Vice President /CMiller@themindfinders.com/ /industries GEN/GOV/NP/positions MIS/NET/TEL/ACC/ADM/TEM
Mr. Amar Greene , Regional Sales Director /AGreene@themindfinders.com/ /industries GEN/GOV/NP/positions MIS/NET/TEL/ACC/ADM/TEM
Ms. Seema Mishra , Director of Strategic Initiatives /SMishra@themindfinders.com/ /industries GEN/GOV/NP/positions MIS/NET/TEL/ACC/ADM/TEM
Mr. Antonio Robertson , Senior Account Executive /ARobertson@themindfinders.com/ /industries GEN/GOV/NP/positions MIS/NET/TEL/ACC/ADM/TEM
Ms. Hilarie Hawley , Account Manager /HHawley@themindfinders.com/ /industries GEN/GOV/NP/positions MIS/NET/TEL/ACC/ADM/TEM
Ms. Ami VandeVelde , Recruiting Manager /AVandeVelde@themindfinders.com/ /industries GEN/GOV/NP/positions MIS/NET/TEL/ACC/ADM/TEM

MITCHELL MARTIN

From the website: Mitchell Martin, Inc. (MMI) is a Talent Acquisition Solutions leader that is powered by innovation and driven by integrity. MMI provides Information Technology staffing, Healthcare staffing and Payroll Solutions nationwide. Founded in 1984, the company initially helped Financial Services companies acquire IT talent in the New York marketplace. Today, MMI has over 1,000 resources deployed across 38 states with annual revenues of $150 million with a diversified client base that includes Insurance, Life Sciences, Technology, Travel, Media and HealthCare.

Minimum salary for assignments: $50,000
Contingency search
Industries: most industries, communications, telecommunications, computers, construction, financial services, healthcare, hospitals, biotechnology, bio-equipment, insurance, manufacturing, services, software e-commerce, internet, new media, travel, broadcasting, media, TV, radio, cable TV
Positions: information technology, MIS, interim, contract, temporary placement
www.mitchellmartin.com

716 South Broadway, 2nd Floor
Baltimore, MD 21231
212-943-1404
Ms. Sarah Martin , Chief Executive Officer /SMartin@itmmi.com

MODIS

From the website: Adecco Technical, a specialty brand of Adecco North America, a division of the world's largest staffing company, has served the technical staffing needs of its clients for almost 50 years. Our nearly 100 offices throughout the U. S. are staffed with recruiters who understand the complexity and diversity of technical disciplines. Coupled with state-of-the-art web-based search and retrieval systems, we can handle all your staffing needs - from the exceptional to the routine. Adecco Technical currently encompasses six vertical employment markets: engineering, information technology, energy, aerospace, creative and scientific, details of which can be found by clicking on the discipline at left. And within each of these markets, we offer a wide variety of types of services.

Minimum salary for assignments: $50,000
Contingency search
Industries: most industries, financial services, insurance, government, public administration, healthcare, hospitals, pharmaceuticals, drugs, biologicals, hospitality, hotels, restaurants, entertainment, film, gaming manufacturing, retail trade, hi-tech, communications, telecommunications, transportation, e-commerce, internet, new media
Positions: information technology, MIS, networks, LAN, WAN, telecommunications, technical, scientific, interim, contract, temporary placement
www.modis.com

6711 Columbia Gateway Drive, Suite 400
Columbia, MD 21046
410-828-0788/fax 410-321-7918
Mr. Dan Gaffney , Managing Director /Daniel.Gaffney@modis.com
Mr. Kernan Kelly , Delivery Director- Government Services /Kernan.Kelly@modis.com/ /industries GOV/positions MIS/NET/TEL/TEC
Ms. Courtney Martin , Division Director /Courtney.Martin@modis.com/ /industries GEN/FIN/INS/GOV/HEA/PHR/positions MIS/NET/TEL/TEC
Mr. Brendan McGowan , Business Development Manager /Brendan.McGowan@modis.com/ /industries GEN/FIN/INS/GOV/HEA/PHR/positions MIS/NET/TEL/TEC
Mr. Ryan McMullen , Business Development Manager /Ryan.McMullen@modis.com/ /industries GEN/FIN/INS/GOV/HEA/PHR/positions MIS/NET/TEL/TEC
Ms. Lauren Crocetti , Resource Development Manager /Lauren.Crocetti@modis.com/ /industries GEN/FIN/INS/GOV/HEA/PHR/positions MIS/NET/TEL/TEC
Mr. Nate Welsh , Resource Development Manager /Nate.Welsh@modis.com/ /industries GEN/FIN/INS/GOV/HEA/PHR/positions MIS/NET/TEL/TEC

NESCO RESOURCE

From the website: Nesco Resource is a leading provider of Staffing Services and HR Solutions, with more than 70 offices throughout the United States. Through our branch office network, we offer our clients and employees services ranging from Temporary Staffing, Permanent Placement, HR Outsourcing and much more. Nesco Resource has dedicated offices supporting Engineering & IT, Clerical & Light Industrial, and Accounting & Finance specialties. Our operating brands also include Lehigh Technical, A-1 Temps, ETS Staffing and DPSS. Nesco Resource is ranked as the

48th largest staffing firm in the United States by Staffing Industry Analysts in 2013, and is ranked as #14 within the Engineering Staffing sector.

Minimum salary for assignments: $40,000
Contingency search
Industries: most industries, banking, healthcare, hospitals, services, manufacturing, financial services, construction, food and beverages, insurance, government, public administration, utilities, transportation wholesale trade, retail trade
Positions: engineering, information technology, MIS, accounting, financial, administration, call centers, manufacturing, industrial labor, logistics management, material management, interim, contract, temporary placement
www.nescoresource.com

43 East South Street
Frederick, MD 21701
301-696-1430
Ms. Stephanie Garcia , Staffing Specialist /SGarcia@nescoresource.com
Ms. Laura Sherman , Recruiter /LSherman@nescoresource.com/ /industries GEN/CON/HEA/SER/MAN/FIN/positions GEN/ADM/ENG/HRS/MAN/MAR

NATIONS EXECUTIVE SEARCH GROUP, INC.

From the website: Nations Executive Search Group (NES Group Inc.) was built to serve the Enterprise Risk Management, Marketing Services and Decision Analytics marketplace. Our specialty includes a blend of retained search for select, high impact senior executive sales and marketing leadership positions and exclusive contingent search for executive level individual contributor sales and marketing positions.

Minimum salary for assignments: $125,000
Contingency search
Industries: direct marketing, financial services, publishing, software, e-commerce, internet, new media
Positions: marketing, sales, senior management
www.nesgroup.net

217 Meadow Avenue
Annapolis, MD 21401
410-827-0180
Mr. Rob Milner , Managing Partner /RMilner@nesgroup.net
Mr. Reece Milner , Business Development Coordinator /RMilner@nesgroup.net/ /industries DIR/FIN/PUB/SFT/WWW/positions MAR/SAL/SEN

ON SEARCH PARTNERS

From the website: With office locations across the country, ON Search Partners has ready access to key executives nationwide, empowering us to discover and recruit the best talent available anywhere. We have extensive experience in conducting C-level searches and in building effective and innovative management teams for our clients in the technology industry. Our in-depth expertise in a continuum of sectors, including energy, cleantech, materials, semiconductor, hardware, software, e-commerce, and life sciences, allows us to confidently deliver consistently superior candidates with the acumen and swiftness your business demands.

Minimum salary for assignments: $100,000
Retained search
Industries: biotechnology, bio-equipment, medical devices, healthcare, hospitals
Positions: most positions, engineering, financial, marketing, manufacturing, information technology, MIS, venture capital, board of directors, senior management
www.onpartners.com

626C Admiral Drive
Annapolis, MD 21401
410-344-7461
Ms. Nina McMaster , Director /Nina@onpartners.com
Mr. Steve Cornacchia , Partner /Steve@onpartners.com/ /industries BIO/MDE/HEA/positions GEN/ENG/FIN/MAR/MAN/MIS

ODGERS BERNDTSON

From the website: Under our global brand, Odgers Berndtson, the group delivers worldwide executive search solutions and is committed to securing exceptional talent to lead and direct the most successful organizations on the planet. Odgers Berndtson is organized in industry and functional practices. Our Industry Practices employ experienced professionals from specific markets areas who are deeply immersed in the target business community - often with a successful industry career behind them. Industry Practices: * Business & Professional Services * Consumer Products & Services * Education * Energy & Utilities * Financial Services * Healthcare * Industrial * Information & Communications * Life Sciences * Media & Entertainment * Public Sector & Not for Profit * Sports * Technology Our Functional Practice experts understand the nuances of successful senior appointments, and provide discrete access to industry leaders. The combination of both disciplines is key in delivering successful candidates for top jobs. Functional practices: * Board & CEO * Corporate Communications * Financial Management * Human Resources * IT Management * Legal * Private Equity * Procurement & Supply Chain

Minimum salary for assignments: $300,000
Retainer/AESC or MAJOR
Industries: healthcare, hospitals, biotechnology, bio-equipment, pharmaceuticals, drugs, biologicals
Positions: most positions, medical, physicians, nurses, therapists, marketing, , regulatory affairs, board of directors
www.odgersberndtson.com

1100 Connecticut Avenue NW
Washington, DC 20036
202-536-5168
Mr. John Hawkins , Vice Chairman, US /John.Hawkins@odgersberndtson.com
Mr. Allen Reed , Partner /Allen.Reed@odgersberndtson.com/ /industries HEA/BIO/PHR/positions GEN/MED/OPS/MAR/RND/REG

Mr. Tim McNamara , Vice Chairman, US /Tim.McNamara@odgersberndtson.com/ /industries AER/DEF/WWW/TRN/CNS/positions GEN/MAR/RND/REG/MIS/BOD
Mr. Derek Wilkinson , Partner /Derek.Wilkinson@odgersberndtson.com/ /industries NP/ED/GOV/positions GEN/MAR/MRE/MIS/RND/BOD
Ms. Linda Kearschner , Principal /Linda.Kearschner@odgersberndtson.com/ /industries TRN/CNS/AER/DEF/SEC/positions GEN/MED/OPS/MAR/RND/REG
Mr. Conrad Woody , Partner /Conrad.Woody@odgersberndtson.com/ /industries GOV/NP/positions GEN/MAR/RND/REG/PRE/SEN

OPTOMI

From the website: At Optomi, we focus on a finite set of skills within the software development lifecycle which allows us to proactively deliver the perfect talent-to-project fit. Our unique company culture values innovation, dedication to our consultants, clients and employees and above all - a philosophy of "doing the right thing". Optomi merges these principles with innovative technologies and industry-leading recruitment processes... allowing us to engage elite talent. We're not your typical IT Staffing firm.

Minimum salary for assignments: $50,000
Contingency search
Industries: most industries, consumer, retail trade, manufacturing, services, hi-tech, government, public administration
Positions: information technology, MIS, networks, LAN, WAN, telecommunications, interim, contract, temporary placement
www.optomi.com

921 East Fort Avenue, Suite 225
Baltimore, MD 21230
410-794-1180
Mr. Chuck Shaffer , Managing Director /ChuckShaffer@optomi.com
Ms. Alyson Smolenski , Account Executive /AlysonSmolenski@optomi.com/ /industries GEN/RTL/MAN/SER/HIT/GOV/positions MIS/NET/TEL/TEM
Mr. Mike LaRoque , Tech Recruiter /MikeLaRoque@optomi.com/ /industries GEN/RTL/MAN/SER/HIT/GOV/positions MIS/NET/TEL/TEM
Ms. Kelli Coughlan , Client Account Manager /KelliCoughlan@optomi.com/ /industries GEN/RTL/MAN/SER/HIT/GOV/positions MIS/NET/TEL/TEM
Mr. Michael Holt , Tech Recruiter /MichaelHolt@optomi.com/ /industries GEN/RTL/MAN/SER/HIT/GOV/positions MIS/NET/TEL/TEM
Ms. Carter Towers , Tech Recruiter /CarterTowers@optomi.com/ /industries GEN/RTL/MAN/SER/HIT/GOV/positions MIS/NET/TEL/TEM

OXEON PARTNERS

From the website: "Oxeon" is the Greek word for relationships. We are inspired by how relationships can drive new jobs, investments, business development opportunities, or just a simple introduction between people. That notion permeates everything we do. We are a healthcare growth services firm. We connect our healthcare company partners with the fundamental drivers of business growth - great people, great business development partnerships, strategic investments, next generation business ideas and other growth-related services.

Minimum salary for assignments: $75,000
Retained search
Industries: healthcare, hospitals
Positions: information technology, MIS, operations, financial
www.oxeonpartners.com

1605 Connecticut Avenue NW, Suite 3
Washington, DC 20009
646-503-2200
Ms. Mia Jung, President /Mia@oxeonpartners.com
Ms. Annah Jamison, Associate /Annah@oxeonpartners.com/ /industries HEA/positions MIS/OPS/FIN
Ms. Margaret Gaby, Senior Associate /Margaret@oxeonpartners.com/ /industries HEA/positions MIS/OPS/FIN
Ms. Fiona Weeks, Senior Associate /Fiona@oxeonpartners.com/ /industries HEA/positions MIS/OPS/FIN

PPS INFORMATION SYSTEMS STAFFING

From the website: PPS Information Systems Staffing provides a comprehensive range of staffing options for every segment of INFORMATION TECHNOLOGY (IT). We can deliver quality people in a timely manner. We fill contractual, temp to perm, and permanent Information technology openings. We specialize in the placement of: * IT Managers * Project Managers * Client Server Developers * Software Developers - .Net, ASP.Net, VB.Net, C#, C++, VB * Database Administrators - Oracle, SQL Server, MySQL, Sybase, Informix, Access * Web Developers - Web Designers, HTML, ASP, Cold Fusion, J2EE, JavaScript * Network Engineers * LAN/WAN Administrators - CISCO, Nortel * Unix Administrators - Solaris, HP-UX, AIX, Linux * Information Security Analysts * Desktop Support Specialists * PC Technicians - Hardware and software support * Help Desk Support Specialists * Clinical IT Analysts.

Minimum salary for assignments: $40,000
Contingency search
Industries: most industries, healthcare, hospitals, communications, telecommunications, information technology, computer services, data processing, hi-tech, software
Positions: information technology, MIS, networks, LAN, WAN, interim, contract, temporary placement
www.ppsinfo.com

1420 East Joppa Road
Towson, MD 21286
410-823-5630/fax 410-821-9423
Mr. Neal Fisher, President /NFisher@ppsinfo.com
Mr. Robert Lanahan, Director of Business Development /RLanahan@ppsinfo.com/ /industries GEN/HEA/CMM/DP/HIT/SFT/positions MIS/NET/TEM

PARTNERSHIP EMPLOYMENT

From the website: Partnership Employment is a Professional Services Firm offering comprehensive Staffing and Search Services. We take staffing to the next level, setting new standards of excellence for both the quality of our candidates and expectations of customer service. We pride ourselves on our ability to consistently deliver the right associate to satisfy your needs, on time, ready to work. We are a full service staffing agency. We represent you to the fullest by finding jobs from limited-term to full-time permanent. We offer a variety of position opportunities in every environment from small and intimate to fortune 500 companies and in both private to public organizations.

No minimum salary for assignments
Contingency search
Industries: most industries
Positions: accounting, financial, information technology, MIS, human resources, administration, interim, contract, temporary placement
www.partnershipemployment.com

1725 I Street, NW
Washington, DC 20006
202-429-1885
Ms. Rachel Amarti , Managing Partner /RAmarti@partnershipemployment.com
Ms. Monica Brumell , Executive Recruiter /MBrumell@partnershipemployment.com/ /industries GEN/positions ACC/FIN/MIS/HRS/ADM/TEM
Mr. Chad Harris , Recruiting Manager /CHarris@partnershipemployment.com/ /industries GEN/positions ACC/FIN/MIS/HRS/ADM/TEM
Ms. Stephanie Bolling , Account Manager /SBolling@partnershipemployment.com/ /industries GEN/positions ACC/FIN/MIS/HRS/ADM/TEM

POTOMAC PARTNERS

From the website: Potomac Partners is one of the Mid-Atlantic region's leading executive search firms providing executive and management level recruitment services in accounting and finance. We have conducted very specialized searches for a variety of industries including financial services, real estate, construction, hospitality, manufacturing, government contracting, non-profit, biotechnology, software, telecommunications, professional services, entertainment/media, and technology. The majority of our searches have been focused in the recruitment of accounting and financial professionals at the management and executive level. Our clients range from high-growth small companies to Fortune 500 global companies. We have executed searches in finance, corporate accounting, financial reporting, accounting policy, treasury, investor relations, tax, financial systems, corporate development, audit, and SOX.

Minimum salary for assignments: $40,000
Contingency search
Industries: most industries, venture capital/private equity, financial services, real estate, construction, hospitality, hotels, restaurants, manufacturing, government, public administration, non-profits biotechnology, bio-equipment, software, communications, telecommunications,

services, entertainment, film, gaming
Positions: financial, accounting, taxes, corporate relations, investor relations, auditing, cash management, interim, contract, temporary placement
www.potomacpartnersllc.com

7315 Wisconsin Avenue, Suite 950W
Bethesda, MD 20814
301-222-1200/fax 301-222-0151
Mr. Mark Williams, Managing Director /MWilliams@potomacpartnersllc.com
Ms. Kimb Crowell, Managing Director /KCrowell@potomacpartnersllc.com/ /industries GEN/positions FIN/ACC/TAX/COR/AUD/CAS
Ms. Maureen Reese, Executive Recruiter /MReese@potomacpartnersllc.com/ /industries GEN/VEN/REA/ENR/FIN/MAN/positions FIN/ACC/TAX/COR/AUD/CAS
Mr. Chris Faha, Director /CFaha@potomacpartnersllc.com/ /industries GEN/VEN/REA/ENR/FIN/MAN/positions FIN/ACC/TAX/COR/AUD/CAS
Mr. Andrew Feldman, Director /AFeldman@potomacpartnersllc.com/ /industries GEN/VEN/REA/ENR/FIN/MAN/positions FIN/ACC/TAX/COR/AUD/CAS
Mr. Timothy Flanagan, Executive Recruiter /TFlanagan@potomacpartnersllc.com/ /industries GEN/VEN/REA/ENR/FIN/MAN/positions FIN/ACC/TAX/COR/AUD/CAS
Ms. Lauren Cherrick, Executive Recruiter /LCherrick@potomacpartnersllc.com/ /industries GEN/MAN/FIN/HSP/REA/RTL/positions FIN/ACC/TAX/COR/AUD/CAS

R.H. PERRY & ASSOCIATES, INC.

From the website: R. H. Perry & Associates (RHPA) is one of the most experienced, and most successful higher education executive search firms in the country. Our firm's primary focus is to assist institutions of higher education in the identification and selection of their leadership.

Minimum salary for assignments: $100,000
Retained search
Industries: education, higher education
Positions: most positions, senior management
www.rhperry.com

2607 31st Street NW
Washington, DC 20008
202-965-6464/fax 202-338-3953
Mr. Bob Perry, President /info@rhperry.com
Mr. Matt Kilcoyne, Managing Partner /Matt@rhperry.com/ /industries ED/positions GEN/SEN
Ms. Judith Perry, Director of Information Technology & Training /JPerry@rhperry.com/ /industries ED/NP/positions GEN/SEN
Mr. John Hutchinson, PhD, Senior Consultant /JohnHutchinson@rhperry.com/ /industries ED/positions GEN/SEN
Ms. Elizabeth Rocklin, Senior Consultant /ERocklin@rhperry.com/ /industries ED/positions GEN/SEN
Mr. Jesse Thompson, Senior Consultant /JesseThompson@rhperry.com/ /industries ED/positions GEN/SEN

RSM US LLP

From the website: RSM US LLP (RSM) is the leading provider of audit, tax and consulting services focused on the middle market, with over 9,000 people in 90 offices nationwide. It is a licensed CPA firm and the U.S. member of RSM International, a global network of independent audit, tax and consulting firms with more than 41,000 people in over 120 countries. RSM uses its deep understanding of the needs and aspirations of clients to help them succeed.

Minimum salary for assignments: $75,000
Retained search
Industries: accounting
Positions: most positions, accounting, auditing, consulting, financial, taxes
www.rsmus.com

100 International Drive
Baltimore, MD 21202
410-246-9300
Mr. Marty Brunk , Office Managing Partner /Marty.Brunk@rsmus.com
Mr. Dominic DuBois , Partner /Dominic.DuBois@rsmus.com/ /industries ACC/positions GEN/ACC/AUD/CNS/FIN/TAX
Mr. Bill Gorman , US Chief Operating Officer /Bill.Gorman@rsmus.com/ /industries ACC/positions GEN/ACC/AUD/CNS/FIN/TAX

5291 Corporate Drive
Frederick, MD 21703
301-663-8600
Ms. Dara Castle , Market Managing Partner /Dara.Castle@rsmus.com

1250 H Street NW
Washington, DC 20005
202-370-8200
Ms. Patti Burquest , Office Managing Partner /Patti.Burquest@rsmus.com
Mr. Dave Kautter , Partner /Dave.Kautter@rsmus.com/ /industries ACC/positions GEN/ACC/AUD/CNS/FIN/TAX

RSR PARTNERS

From the website: RSR Partners is an executive search and corporate governance recruiting firm based in Greenwich, CT. Founded by Russell S. Reynolds, Jr., the founder of Russell Reynolds Associates from which he retired, RSR Partners has been on the leading edge of advising companies through the new corporate governance revolution. The company has confidentially represented companies ranging from Fortune 10 to emerging growth on a variety of leadership issues including CEO succession, board analysis, director recruitment and C-suite executive search. RSR Partners has worked with clients in many industries including financial services, healthcare, consumer products, technology, transportation, automotive and diversified manufacturing. There are three fundamental factors that make a company successful: ideas, capital and people. We supply the most critical and sought after component.

Minimum salary for assignments: $250,000

Retained search
Industries: energy, environmental, green industries, , chemicals, mining, agriculture, agribusiness, industrial
Positions: most positions, logistics management, material management, operations, information technology, MIS, board of directors, senior management
www.rsrpartners.com

One Thomas Circle NW
Washington, DC 20005
202-922-1100
Mr. Christopher Sheeron , Principal /CSheeron@rsrpartners.com

---

RANDSTAD

From the website: Randstad US is a wholly owned subsidiary of Randstad Holding nv, a $22.9 billion global provider of HR services. As the third largest staffing organization in the United States, Randstad provides temporary, temporary-to-hire and permanent placement services each week to over 100,000 people through its network of more than 900 branches and client-dedicated locations. Employing over 5,300 recruiting experts, the company is a top provider of outsourcing, staffing, consulting and projects and workforce solutions within the areas of Engineering, Finance and Accounting, Healthcare, Human Resources, IT, Legal, Manufacturing & Logistics, Office & Administration, Pharma and Sales & Marketing.

No minimum salary for assignments
Contingency search
Industries: most industries, banking, communications, telecommunications, computers, construction, financial services, food and beverages, healthcare, hospitals, hi-tech, manufacturing, services, software e-commerce, internet, new media, transportation
Positions: accounting, auditing, cash management, credit and collections, financial, human resources, logistics management, material management, manufacturing, marketing, , purchasing, sales, taxes, interim, contract, temporary placement
www.randstadusa.com

120 East Baltimore Street, Suite 2220
Baltimore, MD 21202
410-752-5244
Mr. Stephen Wirth , Market Manager /Stephen.Wirth@randstadusa.com
Ms. Katie Boyd , Staffing Manager /Katie.Boyd@randstadusa.com/ /industries GEN/FIN/HEA/MAN/SER/WWW/positions ACC/FIN/HRS/MAN/IND/SAL
Ms. Lauren McGee , Staffing Manager /Lauren.McGee@randstadusa.com/ /industries GEN/FIN/HEA/MAN/SER/WWW/positions ACC/FIN/HRS/MAN/IND/SAL
Ms. Jaclyn Kelbaugh , Staffing Manager /Jaclyn.Kelbaugh@randstadusa.com/ /industries GEN/FIN/HEA/MAN/SER/WWW/positions ACC/FIN/HRS/MAN/IND/SAL

111 Bata Boulevard, Suite B2
Belcamp, MD 21017
410-273-5300
Ms. Lisa Rixham , Senior Account Development Manager /Lisa.Rixham@randstadusa.com
Ms. Karen Mosketti , Recruiter /Karen.Mosketti@randstadusa.com/ /industries GEN/FIN/HEA/MAN/SER/WWW/positions ACC/FIN/HRS/MAN/IND/SAL

Ms. Rachael Shindel , Account Manager /Rachael.Shindel@randstadusa.com/ /industries GEN/FIN/HEA/MAN/SER/WWW/positions ACC/FIN/HRS/MAN/IND/SAL

4330 East West Highway
Bethesda, MD 20814
301-654-7941
Ms. Beth French , Regional Vice President /Elizabeth.French@randstadusa.com
Ms. Katie O'Connor , Staffing Consultant /Katie.OConnor@randstadusa.com/ /industries GEN/FIN/HEA/GOV/SER/WWW/positions ACC/FIN/HRS/MAN/IND/SAL
Mr. Patrick Hopkins , Staffing Manager /Patrick.Hopkins@randstadusa.com/ /industries GEN/FIN/HEA/GOV/SER/WWW/positions ACC/FIN/HRS/MAN/IND/SAL
Ms. Erin von Felden , Executive Recruiter /Erin.vonFelden@randstadusa.com/ /industries GEN/FIN/HEA/GOV/SER/WWW/positions ACC/FIN/HRS/MAN/IND/SAL
Mr. Phillip Nash , Senior Account Executive /Phillip.Nash@randstadusa.com/ /industries GEN/FIN/HEA/GOV/SER/WWW/positions ACC/ADM/FIN/HRS/MAN/SAL
Ms. Christina Tammaro , Staffing Manager /Christina.Tammaro@randstadusa.com/ /industries GEN/FIN/HEA/GOV/SER/WWW/positions ACC/ADM/FIN/HRS/MAN/SAL
Ms. Nicole Dube , Market Manager /Nicole.Dube@randstadusa.com/ /industries GEN/FIN/HEA/GOV/SER/WWW/positions ACC/ADM/FIN/HRS/MAN/SAL

15200 Shady Grove Road
Rockville, MD 20850
301-258-7459
Ms. Beth French , Regional Vice President /Elizabeth.French@randstadusa.com
Ms. Sara Touw , Senior Staffing Consultant /Sara.Touw@randstadusa.com/ /industries GEN/FIN/HEA/MAN/GOV/WWW/positions ACC/ADM/FIN/HRS/IND/SAL
Ms. Katie O'Connor , Staffing Consultant /Katie.OConnor@randstadusa.com/ /industries GEN/FIN/HEA/MAN/GOV/WWW/positions ACC/ADM/FIN/HRS/IND/SAL
Mr. Brian Conley , Executive Recruiter /Brian.Conley@randstadusa.com/ /industries GEN/FIN/HEA/MAN/GOV/WWW/positions ACC/ADM/FIN/HRS/IND/SAL
Mr. Mohammed Yousuff , IT Recruiter /Mohammed.Yousuff@randstadusa.com/ /industries GEN/FIN/HEA/MAN/GOV/WWW/positions MIS/NET/TEL
Mr. Troy Smith , Senior Account Manager /Troy.Smith@randstadusa.com/ /industries GEN/FIN/HEA/MAN/GOV/WWW/positions ACC/ADM/FIN/HRS/IND/SAL

1025 Connecticut Avenue NW, Suite 1201
Washington, DC 20036
202-783-2661
Ms. Nasrine Magaletta , Vice President /Nasrine.Magaletta@randstadusa.com
Ms. Nicole Dube , Market Manager /Nicole.Dube@randstadusa.com/ /industries GEN/FIN/GOV/HEA/MAN/WWW/positions ACC/FIN/HRS/MAN/MAR/SAL
Ms. Sharronne Swann , Senior Staffing Manager /Sharronne.Swann@randstadusa.com/ /industries GEN/FIN/GOV/HEA/MAN/WWW/positions ACC/AUD/CAS/CRE/FIN/TAX
Mr. Nate Fink , Staffing Manager /Nate.Fink@randstadusa.com/ /industries GEN/FIN/GOV/HEA/MAN/WWW/positions ACC/FIN/HRS/MAN/IND/SAL
Mr. Jon Matthews , Business Development Manager /Jon.Matthews@randstadusa.com/ /industries GEN/FIN/GOV/HEA/MAN/WWW/positions ACC/FIN/HRS/MAN/IND/SAL
Ms. Erin von Felden , Executive Recruiter /Erin.vonFelden@randstadusa.com/ /industries GEN/FIN/GOV/HEA/MAN/WWW/positions ACC/FIN/HRS/MAN/IND/SAL
Ms. Doris Jackson , Account Manager /Doris.Jackson@randstadusa.com/ /industries GEN/FIN/GOV/HEA/MAN/WWW/positions ACC/FIN/HRS/MAN/IND/SAL

RANDSTAD PROFESSIONALS

From the website: We are dedicated to helping professionals reach their career goals as well as helping companies build effective staffing strategies. Randstad Professionals is a leading provider of finance, accounting, HR, sales, marketing, and legal staffing and recruitment, providing project, project to direct hire and direct hire services to start-ups, emerging growth and Fortune 500 companies.

Minimum salary for assignments: $25,000
Contingency search
Industries: most industries, government, public administration, banking, financial services, services
Positions: financial, accounting, human resources, sales, marketing, attorneys, paralegals, interim, contract, temporary placement
www.randstadusa.com/professionals

4330 East West Highway, Suite 103
Bethesda, MD 20814
301-654-7941
Ms. Nasrine Magaletta , Vice President /Nasrine.Magaletta@randstadusa.com
Ms. Sharronne Swann , Senior Staffing Manager /Sharronne.Swann@randstadusa.com/ /industries GEN/GOV/BAN/FIN/SER/positions FIN/ACC/HRS/SAL/MAR/LAW
Ms. Kia Powell , Executive Recruiter /Kia.Powell@randstadusa.com/ /industries GEN/GOV/BAN/FIN/SER/positions ACC/AUD/FIN/TAX/CAS/CRE
Mr. Stuart Black , Managing Director /Stuart.Black@randstadusa.com/ /industries GEN/GOV/BAN/FIN/SER/positions FIN/ACC/HRS/SAL/MAR/LAW

RUSSELL REYNOLDS ASSOCIATES

From the website: Whether large or small, public or private, global or local, every company or organization requires an effective leadership team at the top. Finding the right leader for the right position at the right time is a complex challenge best met with the assistance of a firm that has a proven track record of success. Through our worldwide network of 33 offices and more than 275 executive search professionals, Russell Reynolds Associates is committed to earning our clients' trust every day, on every assignment. Our clients benefit from our unmatched expertise in executive search and assessment and our unique, collaborative, "one-firm" approach designed to quickly identify the highest-quality candidates worldwide

Minimum salary for assignments: $200,000
Retainer/AESC or MAJOR
Industries: most industries, non-profits, healthcare, hospitals, biotechnology, bio-equipment, government, public administration, broadcasting, media, TV, radio, cable TV, communications, telecommunications, aerospace defense, venture capital/private equity
Positions: most positions, board of directors, financial, attorneys, paralegals, manufacturing, information technology, MIS, market research, product research, , senior management, technical, scientific
www.russellreynolds.com

1700 New York Avenue NW

Washington, DC 20006-5208
202-654-7800
Ms. Kimberly Archer , Consultant /Kimberly.Archer@russellreynolds.com
Ms. Mercedes LeGrand , Consultant /Mercedes.LeGrand@russellreynolds.com/ /industries HIT/IND/NAT/DEF/GOV/CMM/positions GEN/MIS/MAR/HRS/SEN
Ms. Jamie Hechinger , Managing Director /Jamie.Hechinger@russellreynolds.com/ /industries HEA/PHR/BIO/NP/positions GEN/SEN/MIS/AFF
Mr. Will McKinnon , Consultant /William.McKinnon@russellreynolds.com/ /industries HIT/CMM/ACC/LAW/positions GEN/SEN/MIS/SEC/HRS/ENG
Ms. Stephanie Tomasso , Consultant /Stephanie.Tomasso@russellreynolds.com/ /industries HEA/NP/ED/positions GEN/REG/COR/DEV/AFF/SEN
Ms. Mary Tydings , Managing Director /Mary.Tydings@russellreynolds.com/ /industries NP/ED/positions GEN/COR/DEV/SEN
Mr. Jett Pihakis , Consultant /Jett.Pihakis@russellreynolds.com/ /industries NP/ED/positions FIN/MIS/AFF

SNI COMPANIES

From the website: SNI Companies(r) is a premier provider of recruitment and staffing services specializing in administrative, finance, accounting, banking, technology, and legal professions. We deliver staffing solutions across a wide range of disciplines and industries: >> Staffing Now(r) specializes in matching administrative professionals with the right temporary and temp-to-hire opportunities in a variety of clients in all industries. SNI Administrative(r) specializes in full-time clerical and administrative recruitment. >> Accounting Now(r) specializes in matching financial professionals with the right contract or contract-to-hire opportunities in finance, accounting and banking. Its sister division, SNI Financial(r), specializes in full-time accounting and finance recruitment. >> SNI Technology(r) offers technical talent and employment opportunities on a contract, contract-to-hire, and a full-time basis in a wide variety of disciplines from helpdesk professionals to the most cutting-edge software architects. >> Legal Now(r) focuses on matching legal professionals with the right law firms and corporate law departments on contract and contract-to-hire arrangements. Its sister division, SNI Legal(r) matches legal experts and employers on a direct-hire basis.

No minimum salary for assignments
Contingency search
Industries: most industries, healthcare, hospitals, law firms, manufacturing
Positions: accounting, administration, call centers, financial, attorneys, paralegals, information technology, MIS, interim, contract, temporary placement
www.snicompanies.com

51 Monroe Street, Suite PW02
Rockville, MD 20850
301-565-4353/fax 301-565-8171
Mr. Kevin Jones , Managing Director /KJones@snicompanies.com
Ms. Mona Bass , Staffing Manager /MBass@snicompanies.com/ /industries GEN/HEA/LAW/MAN/positions ACC/ADM/CAL/FIN/LAW/MIS
Ms. Angela Ponce de Leon , Staffing Manager /APoncedeLeon@snicompanies.com/ /industries GEN/HEA/LAW/MAN/positions ACC/ADM/CAL/FIN/LAW/MIS

SANFORD ROSE ASSOCIATES - ANNAPOLIS

From the website: Sanford Rose Associates - Annapolis focuses on retained level and exclusive contingency searches in two practice areas: SPECIALTY CHEMICALS and FORMULATED AND CONVERTED PRODUCTS which are based on specialty chemicals.
Minimum salary for assignments: $75,000
Retained search
Industries: chemicals, biotechnology, bio-equipment
Positions: most positions, marketing, information technology, MIS, , sales
www.sanfordrose.com/annapolis

721 Main Street
Stevensville, MD 21666
410-604-3370
Mr. Pete Norton , Managing Partner /PANorton@sanfordrose.com
Ms. Eleni Mioduszewski , Lead Executive Recruiter /EKMioduszewski@sanfordrose.com/ /industries CHM/BIO/positions GEN/MAR/MIS/RND/SAL
Ms. Tina Damron , Lead Executive Recruiter /TMDamron@sanfordrose.com/ /industries CHM/BIO/positions GEN/MAR/MIS/RND/SAL
Mr. David Felker, PhD , Senior Executive Search Advisor /DFelker@sanfordrose.com/ /industries CHM/BIO/positions GEN/MAR/MIS/RND/SAL
Mr. Leonard Sarkissian , Partner & Executive Search Consultant /LSarkissian@sanfordrose.com/ /industries CHM/BIO/positions GEN/MAR/MIS/RND/SAL

SAVOY PARTNERS LTD.

From the website: Founded in 1980 by senior executive search professionals, Savoy Partners is consistently among the Top Ten executive search firms based in the Greater Washington area. The firm conducts senior level retained searches, typically for Presidents or positions that report to a President. While most of its larger competitors use associates and research assistants and rely increasingly on databases or the Internet, Savoy continues to perform all searches at the Partner level. We rarely fail.

Minimum salary for assignments: $125,000
Retainer/AESC or MAJOR
Industries: most industries, hi-tech, consumer, financial services, communications, telecommunications, aerospace, defense, government, public administration, security services and products, venture capital/private equity
Positions: most positions, accounting, financial, international, marketing, information technology, MIS, sales, senior management, telecommunications
www.savoypartners.com

3900 Cathedral Avenue NW, #312A
Washington, DC 20016
202-887-0666
Mr. Robert J. Brudno , Managing Director /RBrudno@savoypartners.com

SPENCER STUART

From the website: Leadership requirements continue to evolve, but the need for high-performing executives remains constant. Identifying and attracting this talent requires a rigorous approach, a thorough understanding of different industries and functional roles, unrivaled access to senior executives and impeccable judgment. Spencer Stuart consultants apply real insight into clients' strategic requirements and proven assessment tools to recruit leaders who have the necessary skill, experience and personal qualities to advance company strategies and achieve outstanding results We have a far-reaching network of relationships with top executives across all industries, giving us an expansive view of nearly 3 million leaders in every function and sector of business. Executives trust us to bring them opportunities that represent a good fit with their capabilities and ambitions. Our practices are at the heart of our approach to search. Spencer Stuart professionals belong to industry and functional practices according to their experience and expertise. Through these practices we pool our sector and candidate knowledge and conduct focused research on talent and industry trends. >> Industries: * Business & Professional Services * Consumer * Education, Nonprofit & Government * Energy * Financial Services * Industrial * Life Sciences * Private Equity * Technology, Media & Telecommunications >> Functions: * Boards * Chief Executive Officer * Financial Officer * Human Resources * Information Officer * Legal, Compliance & Regulatory * Marketing Officer * Supply Chain >> Areas of Expertise: * Corporate Communications * Digital, E-Commerce & Transformative Technologies * Diversity * Family Business * Sales Officer

Minimum salary for assignments: $150,000
Retainer/AESC or MAJOR
Industries: most industries, services, consumer, non-profits, government, public administration, energy, financial services, industrial, biotechnology, bio-equipment, venture capital/private equity, hi-tech, broadcasting, media, TV, radio, cable TV communications, telecommunications, e-commerce, internet, new media
Positions: most positions, board of directors, senior management, financial, human resources, information technology, MIS, attorneys, paralegals, regulatory affairs, marketing, logistics management, material management purchasing, international, diversity, multicultural, affirmative action, sales
www.spencerstuart.com

799 9th Street NW
Washington, DC 20001
202-639-8111
Ms. Leslie Hortum , Consultant and Partner /LHortum@spencerstuart.com
Ms. Jackie Arends , Consultant /JGArends@spencerstuart.com/ /industries AER/DEF/NP/ED/GOV/IND/positions SEN/LAW/REG/MAR
Ms. Liz Moulton , Consultant, Co-Leader US Sports Practice /EMoulton@spencerstuart.com/ /industries CON/SPO/ENT/positions GEN/MAR/BOD/SEN
Ms. Ana Rhea , Consultant /ARhea@spencerstuart.com/ /industries SER/BRO/CMM/positions GEN/MAR/BOD/SEN
Mr. David Wick , Consultant /DWick@spencerstuart.com/ /industries ED/NP/GOV/positions GEN/DEV/SEN
Ms. Courtney Fletcher , Consultant /CFletcher@spencerstuart.com/ /industries GEN/CON/GOV/FIN/HIT/WWW/positions FIN/REG
Ms. Louise Huang , Consultant /LHuang@spencerstuart.com/ /industries HSP/LEI/positions GEN/MAR/SAL/FIN/MIS/SEN

STAFFMARK

From the website: We recognize that you have choices when it comes to staffing companies. What makes Staffmark different? We think it's our focus on two things: people and results. This focus has allowed Staffmark to create one of the top customer satisfaction programs in the staffing industry. Staffmark has been named to Inavero's 2012 Best of Staffing Client list. Fewer than 1% of North American staffing firms have been named to the 2012 Best of Staffing Client list. Specialties: Accounting and Finance, Administrative and Office, Call Center, Electronics, Engineering, Health Care and Medical Office, Industrial, Information Technology, Legal, Logistics, Mortgage and Transportation

No minimum salary for assignments
Contingency search
Industries: most industries, banking, financial services, biotechnology, bio-equipment, pharmaceuticals, drugs, biologicals, computers, software, consulting, management consulting, consumer, food and beverages, insurance e-commerce, internet, new media, utilities, retail trade
Positions: most positions, accounting, administration, call centers, financial, human resources, industrial labor, information technology, MIS, interim, contract, temporary placement
www.staffmark.com

6 West Washington Street
Hagerstown, MD 21740
240-313-9100
Mr. David Lakner, Branch Manager /David.Lakner@staffmark.com

STANTON CHASE

From the website: Stanton Chase is a global executive search firm that partners with leading businesses, governments, non-governmental organizations and not-for-profits to assess and acquire top executive leadership talent to drive breakthrough performance. We are proud of our widespread executive search group: our Global Industry Specialization Groups feature members with expertise in every major industry while our Functional Specialty Practice Groups provide extraordinary competencies in our leadership consultation services.

Minimum salary for assignments: $125,000
Retainer/AESC or MAJOR
Industries: most industries, consumer, financial services, biotechnology, bio-equipment, healthcare, hospitals, industrial, hi-tech, government, public administration, education, higher education, non-profits, natural resources energy, services
Positions: most positions, diversity, multicultural, affirmative action, automation, cash management, engineering, human resources, international, manufacturing, marketing, medical, physicians, nurses, therapists, quality, senior management, technical, scientific
www.stantonchase.com

400 East Pratt Street
Baltimore, MD 21202
410-528-8400

Mr. Ted Muendel, Managing Director /T.Muendel@stantonchase.com
Mr. Mickey Matthews, International Chairman / Managing Director
/M.Matthews@stantonchase.com/ /industries IND/CON/positions
GEN/FIN/MAR/ENG/MAN/OPS
Mr. James Paxton, Senior Director, Healthcare /J.Paxton@stantonchase.com/ /industries
HEA/BIO/MDE/PHR/positions GEN/FIN/MAR/ENG/MAN/OPS
Mr. Donald Davidson, Director /D.Davidson@stantonchase.com/ /industries
BIO/HEA/PHR/positions GEN/FIN/MAR/ENG/MAN/OPS
Ms. Lyn Cason, Global Sector Leader - Advertising, /L.Cason@stantonchase.com/ /industries
CON/GOV/NP/ADV/BRO/PUB/positions ADV/FIN/HRS/AFF
Mr. David Ptak, Director /D.Ptak@stantonchase.com/ /industries FIN/BIO/HEA/MDE/positions
GEN/FIN/MAR/MAN/OPS/VEN
Ms. Margaret Bonanno-Paa, Director of Research /M.Bonanno-Paa@stantonchase.com/
/industries GEN/HIT/HEA/FIN/CON/IND/positions GEN/FIN/MAR/ENG/MAN/OPS

10 G Street NE
Washington, DC 20002
202-248-5088
Ms. Lyn Cason, Managing Director /L.Cason@stantonchase.com
Mr. Jeff Perkins, Advisory Director /J.Perkins@stantonchase.com/ /industries
HIT/BRO/WWW/GOV/ED/NP/positions GEN/FIN/MAR/ENG/MAN/LOG
Mr. Mickey Matthews, Managing Director /M.Matthews@stantonchase.com/ /industries
GEN/IND/CON/positions GEN/FIN/MAR/ENG/MAN/LOG
Ms. Kathleen Hajek, Director /K.Hajek@stantonchase.com/ /industries
BIO/HEA/GOV/ED/NP/VEN/positions GEN/AFF/HRS/BOD
Mr. Charles Nailen, Director /C.Nailen@stantonchase.com/ /industries
AER/HIT/WWW/positions GEN/FIN/MAR/ENG/MIS/LOG

STARTFINDER

From the website: StartFinder is a recruitment outsourcing business that provides co-sourcing solutions to help Talent Acquisition leaders build world-class organizations. Our clients include big four management consulting businesses, Fortune 500 companies and some of the world's most famous technology companies. We are also the parent company of CIO Resources (www.cioresources.com) a management consulting firm that helps Information Technology leaders.

Minimum salary for assignments: $50,000
Contingency search
Industries: most industries
Positions: information technology, MIS, networks, LAN, WAN, interim, contract, temporary placement
www.startfinder.com

2275 Research Boulevard, Suite 500
Rockville, MD 20850
240-668-4844
Mr. Doug Roper, Partner /Doug@startfinder.com
Mr. Alan Strauss, Managing Partner /Alan@startfinder.com/ /industries GEN/positions
MIS/NET/TEM

Ms. Stefany Goldberg , Senior Recruiter /Stefany@startfinder.com/ /industries GEN/positions HRS
Ms. Kim Roszel , Senior Associate /Kim@startfinder.com/ /industries GEN/positions HRS
Ms. Karen Fisher , Senior Associate /Karen@startfinder.com/ /industries GEN/positions MIS/NET/TEM
Mr. Barry Smith , Managing Partner /Barry@startfinder.com/ /industries GEN/positions MIS/NET/TEM
Ms. Jenna Kolesky , Senior Account Manager /Jenna@startfinder.com/ /industries GEN/positions MIS/NET/TEM

STERLING MARTIN ASSOCIATES

From the website: Founded in 2006, Sterling Martin Associates (SMA) is a leading executive search firm that focuses on finding talented leaders for the nation's associations and nonprofit organizations. Over the last seven years, Sterling Martin Associates has been engaged by nearly 100 clients throughout the United States; our staff consists of 15 professionals located in Washington, DC, New York, NY, San Francisco, CA, and Costa Mesa, CA.

Minimum salary for assignments: $75,000
Retained search
Industries: non-profits
Positions: senior management, board of directors, development, fund raising
www.smartinsearch.com

1025 Connecticut Avenue NW
Washington, DC 20036
202-327-5485/fax 202-857-9799
Mr. David Martin , CEO and Managing Partner /DMartin@smartinsearch.com
Ms. Virginia Record , Director of Search Management /VRecord@smartinsearch.com/ /industries NP/positions SEN/BOD/DEV
Ms. Erin Lawrence , Director of Marketing & Research /Erin@smartinsearch.com/ /industries NP/positions SEN/BOD/DEV
Ms. Tricia Canavan , Senior Consultant /TCanavan@smartinsearch.com/ /industries NP/positions SEN/BOD/DEV
Ms. Karen Lombardo , Senior Associate /KLombardo@smartinsearch.com/ /industries NP/positions SEN/BOD/DEV
Ms. Jessica Champion , Research Associate /JChampion@smartinsearch.com/ /industries NP/positions SEN/BOD/DEV

STEVEN DOUGLAS ASSOCIATES

From the website: Steven Douglas Associates, one of the nation's leading boutique search and project-based firms, has been a recognized leader in identifying and providing access to top talent for corporate clients since 1984. Our client base is industry agnostic and ranges from start-ups and emerging middle-market to Fortune 500 companies and private equity firms. Vertical specialization by practice area allows our consultants a deep grounding and knowledge of these specific markets: * Financial Services * Corporate Information Technology * Accounting And Finance * Health Care * Supply Chain Management - Diversity * International * Human Resources * Legal * Not-For-Profit/Foundations. Specialties * Finance & Accounting, * Financial Services, * Information Technology, * Sales, Marketing & Operations, * Human Resources, * Healthcare & Life Sciences.

Minimum salary for assignments: $100,000
Contingency search
Industries: most industries, accounting, financial services, healthcare, hospitals, investment banks, merchant banks, manufacturing, non-profits, real estate, services
Positions: most positions, accounting, engineering, financial, human resources, , manufacturing, marketing, information technology, MIS, quality, sales, senior management, taxes, interim, contract, temporary placement
www.stevendouglas.com

3700 O'Donnell Street
Baltimore, MD 21224
443-438-6599
Mr. Matthew Beck , Vice President /MBeck@stevendouglas.com

STORBECK/PIMENTEL & ASSOCIATES

From the website: Storbeck/Pimentel & Associates is a retained executive search firm, specializing in higher education executive recruitment for colleges and universities, with additional practices in independent school and nonprofit recruitment. Our mission is to find the best leaders uniquely suited to address the needs of our clients while providing the highest levels of service and collaboration.

Minimum salary for assignments: $150,000
Retainer/AESC or MAJOR
Industries: education, higher education, non-profits
Positions: most positions, diversity, multicultural, affirmative action, board of directors, development, fund raising, training, education, financial, marketing, senior management
www.storbeckpimentel.com

Baltimore, MD
410-243-1012
Ms. Susan May , Partner /S.May@storbecksearch.com

Washington, DC
484-263-5518
Mr. Jim Sirianni, PhD , Principal /J.Sirianni@storbeckpimentel.com

---

TALASCEND

From the website: For over 60 years, Talascend has been at the leading edge of resourcing solutions in the technical sector. We provide projects and companies across the industry with tactical and strategic resourcing options. In a market where demand for skills is high and supply low, we are helping our customers to connect with the right people and companies for them - connecting hiring managers, HR strategists and technical professionals and most importantly - putting people to work.

Minimum salary for assignments: $50,000
Contingency search
Industries: , transportation, automotive, motor vehicles, trucks, communications, telecommunications, energy, defense, mining, aerospace, boats, marine products and services, healthcare, hospitals
Positions: engineering, manufacturing, information technology, MIS, safety, human resources, quality, industrial labor, interim, contract, temporary placement
www.talascend.com

321 Ballenger Center Drive, Suite 245
Frederick, MD 21703
301-663-9220/fax 856-494-1405
Mr. Josh Kaplan , Senior Vice President /Josh.Kaplan@talascend.com
Ms. Erin Miller , Technical Recruiter /Erin.Miller@talascend.com/ /industries ONG/TRN/AUT/CMM/ENR/DEF/positions ENG/MAN/TEM
Mr. Ron Wood , Chief Executive Officer /Ron.Wood@talascend.com/ /industries ONG/TRN/AUT/CMM/ENR/DEF/positions ENG/MIS/QUA/TEM
Ms. Liza Richards , Senior Technical Recruiter /Liza.Richards@talascend.com/ /industries ONG/TRN/AUT/CMM/ENR/DEF/positions ENG/MIS/QUA/TEM
Ms. Meagan Lynch , Recruiter /Meagan.Lynch@talascend.com/ /industries ONG/TRN/AUT/CMM/ENR/DEF/positions ENG/MAN/MIS/SAF/HRS/IND
Ms. Billie Jo McTighe , Lead Technical Recruiter - Northeast /BillieJo.McTighe@talascend.com/ /industries ONG/TRN/AUT/CMM/ENR/DEF/positions ENG/MIS/QUA/TEM
Ms. Melissa Hienkle , Account Executive /Melissa.Hienkle@talascend.com/ /industries ONG/TRN/AUT/CMM/ENR/DEF/positions MIS/NET

TECHNOLOGY EXECUTIVE GROUP

*From the website: At Technology Executive Group we believe the world continues to become more specialized every day. To support this ongoing trend, we have organized our company into niche practices within the technology sector. We expect our search consultants to have a deep understanding of the business climate in their respective areas. This precise focus allows us to uncover valuable knowledge for our clients and also develop a mutually respected relationship with the "A" players in each practice area. Practices: * Communications Services * Communication Systems & Software * IT Services & Solutions * Wireless & Mobility*

Minimum salary for assignments: $75,000
Contingency search
Industries: communications, telecommunications, software, wireless communications, e-commerce, internet, new media
Positions: most positions, financial, information technology, MIS, sales, marketing, engineering, operations, senior management
www.tegexecutive.com

5221 Baltimore Avenue
Bethesda, MD 20816
240-235-6028
Ms. Kristin Wardour , Principal /KWardour@tegexecutive.com
Ms. Ethel Dailey , Research Associate /EDailey@tegexecutive.com/ /industries
CMM/SFT/WIR/WWW/positions GEN/FIN/MIS/SAL/MAR/ENG
Ms. Carol Barker , Principal /CBarker@tegexecutive.com/ /industries
CMM/SFT/WIR/WWW/positions GEN/FIN/MIS/SAL/MAR/ENG
Ms. Jill Greenblat , Principal /JGreenblat@tegexecutive.com/ /industries
CMM/SFT/WIR/WWW/positions GEN/FIN/MIS/SAL/MAR/ENG
Ms. Sarah McCullough , Partner /SMcCullough@tegexecutive.com/ /industries
CMM/SFT/WIR/WWW/positions GEN/FIN/MIS/SAL/MAR/ENG
MS. Stefanie Good , Research Specialist /SGood@tegexecutive.com/ /industries
CMM/SFT/WIR/WWW/positions GEN/FIN/MIS/SAL/MAR/ENG

TRIUMPH SEARCH CONSULTANTS, INC.

From the website: Triumph Search Consultants the premier attorney placement firm for 14 years. We introduce outstanding candidates to the right opportunities with a variety of legal employers. We have experience working with partners, associates and groups of attorneys to find the right fit. We work with most major national and international law firms, and have contacts in numerous other cities throughout the U.S. and the world.

Minimum salary for assignments: $75,000
Contingency search
Industries: most industries, law firms
Positions: attorneys, paralegals
www.triumphsearch.com

1808 Swann Street NW
Washington, DC 20009
202-652-1793
Mr. Evan Goldberg , Esq. , Recruiter /Evan@triumphsearch.com
Mr. Richard Kanter, Esq. , Recruiter /Richard@triumphsearch.com/ /industries GEN/LAW/positions LAW
Ms. Erica Schwitzer, Esq. , Recruiter /Erica@triumphsearch.com/ /industries GEN/LAW/positions LAW

VETTED SOLUTIONS

From the website: Vetted Solutions has become the trusted partner of a growing roster of associations and nonprofits by delivering consistently superior search results. Our approach produces truly better candidates, capable of both making immediate contributions to exceptional organizational performance and providing the lasting leadership that drives significant sustained results.

Minimum salary for assignments: $100,000
Retainer/AESC or MAJOR
Industries: non-profits
Positions: board of directors, senior management, interim, contract, temporary placement
www.vettedsolutions.com

1101 14th Street NW
Washington, DC 20005
202-544-4749
Mr. Jim Zaniello , President / CEO /Jim.Zaniello@vettedsolutions.com
Ms. Evelyn Savage , Vice President /Evelyn.Savage@vettedsolutions.com/ /industries NP/positions BOD/SEN/TEM
Ms. Judith Walker , Vice President /Judy.Walker@vettedsolutions.com/ /industries NP/positions BOD/SEN/TEM
Ms. Kristan McMahon , Principal /Kristan@vettedsolutions.com/ /industries NP/positions BOD/SEN/TEM
Ms. Lynette Dennis , Project Manager /Lynette@vettedsolutions.com/ /industries NP/positions BOD/SEN/TEM
Ms. Amy Weist , Search Manager /Amy@vettedsolutions.com/ /industries NP/positions BOD/SEN/TEM
Ms. Brittany Bayliss , Consultant /Brittany@vettedsolutions.com/ /industries NP/positions BOD/SEN/TEM

WARD HOWELL INTERNATIONAL

From the website: Ward Howell International aspires to be the most reputable global leadership consulting firm, recognized as preeminent in developing partnerships with our clients that consistently exceed their expectations. Our distinctiveness derives from the quality of our people who share values of entrepreneurship, in depth local expertise, and international collaboration and perspective. Practices: * Automotive * Consumer * Financial Services * Industrial * Legal * Life Science * Luxury * Media * Retail * Technology * Interim.

Minimum salary for assignments: $100,000
Retainer/AESC or MAJOR
Industries: most industries, automotive, motor vehicles, trucks, financial services, industrial, law firms, biotechnology, bio-equipment, broadcasting, media, TV, radio, cable TV, consumer, retail trade, hi-tech, communications, telecommunications wireless communications, e-commerce, internet, new media
Positions: most positions, human resources, sales, marketing, logistics management, material management, accounting, financial, engineering, manufacturing, senior management, interim, contract, temporary placement
www.ward-howell.com

12309 Brookhaven Drive
Silver Spring, MD 20902
248-719-3125
Mr. S. Qaisar Shareef , Advisory Partner /silverspring@ward-howell.com

WEGMAN PARTNERS

From the website: The foremost local and national law firms and corporations rely on Wegman Partners as their primary source for attorneys and legal support staff. We provide a recognized expertise in assessing the talents and goals of our candidates and guide them throughout the process of their career development. We do this by introducing our candidates to our prestigious clients, listening to their perceptions and requirements, and providing our objective advice and constant support. In addition to our existing clientele, our staff continually develops new relationships within the national legal market for the purpose of identifying new career opportunities for our candidates.

Minimum salary for assignments: $75,000
Contingency search
Industries: most industries, law firms
Positions: attorneys, paralegals
www.wegmanpartners.com

Baltimore, MD
410-294-9936
Ms. Jordan Kline Parrish , Director of Legal Recruiting /JParrish@wegmanpartners.com

2101 L St NW
Washington, DC 20037
202-903-0744
Ms. Cheryl Brown, Esq. , Managing Director /CBrown@wegmanpartners.com
Ms. Sara Young, Esq. , Director of Legal Recruiting /SYoung@wegmanpartners.com/ /industries GEN/LAW/positions LAW
Ms. Jordan Kline Parrish , Director of Legal Recruiting /JParrish@wegmanpartners.com/ /industries GEN/LAW/positions LAW
Ms. Diana Rubin, Esq. , Managing Director /DRubin@wegmanpartners.com/ /industries GEN/LAW/positions LAW

WITT/KIEFFER

From the website: Witt/Kieffer serves hospitals, health systems, academic medical centers and other health-related organizations; life sciences companies including pharmaceutical, biotech, diagnostics and medical device corporations; colleges and universities and not-for-profit community service organizations and foundations. Our clients have relied on Witt/Kieffer for 40 years to identify leaders with the best mix of skills, experience, vision and character to fulfill their missions. For them and for us, executive search is about much more than filling a chair - It's about bringing great leadership to your organization.

Minimum salary for assignments: $100,000
Retainer/AESC or MAJOR
Industries: education, higher education, healthcare, hospitals
Positions: most positions, development, fund raising, human resources, physicians, senior

management, interim, contract, temporary placement
www.wittkieffer.com

1340 Smith Avenue
Baltimore, MD 21209
410-779-1250
Mr. Philip Tang , Consultant /PTang@wittkieffer.com

7250 Woodmont Avenue
Bethesda, MD 20814
301-654-5070/fax 301-654-1318
Mr. Oliver Tomlin , Senior Partner /OTomlin@wittkieffer.com
Ms. Jennifer Bauer , Consultant /JenniferB@wittkieffer.com/ /industries HEA/ED/NP/positions GEN/DEV/HRS/PHY/SEN
Ms. Rachel Polhemus , Senior Partner /RachelP@wittkieffer.com/ /industries HEA/positions GEN/DEV/HRS/PHY/SEN
Ms. Anna Wharton Phillips , Of Counsel Advisor /AnnaP@wittkieffer.com/ /industries ED/HEA/MCA/NP/PHR/positions GEN/DEV/HRS/PHY/SEN
Mr. Daniel Dimenstein , Associate /DDimenstein@wittkieffer.com/ /industries HEA/ED/positions GEN/DEV/HRS/PHY/SEN
Ms. Ann Yates , Principal /AYates@wittkieffer.com/ /industries ED/positions GEN/DEV/HRS/PHY/SEN

ZRG PARTNERS

From the website: ZRG Partners, LLC is a revolutionized talent management provider. We provide senior-level executive search services grounded in our DNA that values data and analytics in conjunction with great search process. Our proprietary Z score process helps clients make informed hiring decisions while avoiding costly hiring mistakes. ZRG Partners delivers a wide range of executive search solutions grounded in the work we have done with clients and listening to their needs before delivering innovative, fact-based solutions to solve their specific dilemma. We understand that in order for organizations to thrive, they need leadership that fits into the company culture.

Minimum salary for assignments: $100,000
Retained search
Industries: aerospace, consumer, education, higher education, financial services, healthcare, hospitals, industrial, biotechnology, bio-equipment, non-profits, venture capital/private equity, hi-tech e-commerce, internet, new media
Positions: most positions, board of directors, financial, information technology, MIS, marketing, sales, senior management, international
www.zrgpartners.com

2200 Pennsylvania Avenue NW
Washington, DC 20037
202-386-9000
Ms. Phoebe Henderson , Managing Director /PHenderson@zrgpartners.com
Mr. Rich Herman , Managing Director /RHerman@zrgpartners.com/ /industries FIN/VEN/positions GEN/BOD/FIN/MAR/SAL/SEN
Mr. David Fortier , Managing Partner /DFortier@zrgpartners.com/ /industries

BIO/PHR/MDE/HEA/positions GEN/BOD/FIN/MAR/SAL/SEN
Mr. Kerry Moynihan , Managing Director /KMoynihan@zrgpartners.com/ /industries GEN/CON/FIN/HEA/HIT/WWW/positions GEN/FIN/MIS/MAR/SAL/INT

Chapter 3: Appendix - Note

AESC or MAJOR -- These are executive search firms which are large retainer-only generalist firms or are members of the Association of Executive Search Consultants (AESC) which are generalist firms. These firms are large enough to have assignments in specific areas, but may indicate only general for their industry or position specialties.

Chapter 4: Appendix - About The Data

The data supplied in this Directory have been compiled by surveying the companies in the database by phone and by mail and on the internet. Data are updated on a continuing basis, but frequency is not assured. Because of the possibility of error by its sources, Custom Databanks, Inc. does not warrant for the accuracy, errors, omissions or adverse consequences to anyone resulting from use or reliance upon such data. No endorsement, rating or qualification of any company is implied by its inclusion in the data supplied by this software.

This Directory is sold subject to the condition that it shall not, by way of trade or otherwise, be lent, resold, hired our or otherwise circulated without the publisher's prior consent in any form whatsoever. You may not make any changes or modifications to this Directory or the data contained herein. You may not decompile, disassemble, or otherwise reverse engineer this Directory. You may not sub-license, rent, lend, lease, donate, sell, load, pledge, transfer, or distribute on a temporary or permanent basis any of the data contained in this Directory to another person or company.

Title to this Directory and the data which it makes available is retained by Custom Databanks, Inc. and is not transferred to any user by grant of a license as provided. **You may not sell or further license this Directory or its data to any other person or organization without the express written permission of Custom Databanks, Inc.**

Copyright © 2020 Custom Databanks, Inc. All Rights Reserved

CPSIA information can be obtained
at www.ICGtesting.com
Printed in the USA
BVHW030813150320
575052BV00001B/79